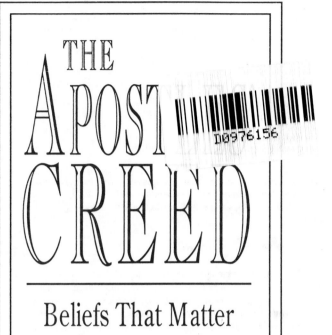

THE
APOSTLES'
CREED

Beliefs That Matter

STUART BRISCOE

Harold Shaw Publishers
Wheaton, Illinois

ISBN 0-87788-052-2

Cover design by David LaPlaca

Library of Congress Cataloging-in-Publication Data

Briscoe, Stuart D.
   Apostles' Creed : beliefs that matter / Stuart Briscoe.
     p. cm.
   ISBN 0-87788-052-2
   1. Apostles' Creed. I. Title.
  BT993.2.B645 1994
  238'.11—dc20   93-41884
                                               CIP

99 98 97 96 95 94

10 9 8 7 6 5 4 3 2 1

Contents

The Apostles' Creed

I believe in God the Father Almighty,
   Maker of heaven and earth;
And in Jesus Christ his only Son our Lord;
   who was conceived by the Holy Spirit,
   born of the Virgin Mary,
   suffered under Pontius Pilate,
   was crucified, dead, and buried;
   and descended into Hades.
   The third day he rose again from the dead.
   He ascended into heaven,
   and sitteth on the right hand of God the Father Almighty.
   Whence he shall come to judge the quick and the dead.
I believe in the Holy Spirit;
   the holy catholic church;
   the communion of saints;
   the forgiveness of sins;
   the resurrection of the body;
   and the life everlasting.
  Amen.

1

Does What You Believe Really Matter?

Romans 4:17-25

About a hundred and fifty years ago Alexis de Tocqueville, a French sociologist, visited the United States and then returned home to write a book called *Democracy in America,* a book that it seems nobody has read but everybody quotes from. One of the expressions he used in that book was "the habits of the heart." By that he meant social mores, the reasons behind why people act the way they do.

More recently, another sociologist, Robert Bellah, has written a book entitled *Habits of the Heart,* in which he examines American society to find out what makes it tick. He was particularly interested in American belief systems, and he made some startling discoveries. One of the people he interviewed, Sheila, had this to say: "I believe in God. I can't remember the last time I went to church, but my faith has carried me a long way." Bellah felt her words characterize the attitudes of many people and called it "Sheilaism."

Gods of our own imagination

Surveys in America show that 80 percent of Americans believe in God, but when you look carefully into the "god" in whom they believe, you find "Sheilaism." Many Americans claim to believe in

God, but in actual fact they really are listening to a little voice inside themselves.

Chuck Colson commented on this as follows:

When the not-so-still or small voice of the self becomes the highest authority, religious belief undergoes a change so dramatic that it no longer involves commitment to any authority beyond one's self. The church is no longer regarded as a repository of truth, nor as a source of moral authority, but merely as a place to go for spiritual strokes.

I think he has hit the nail firmly on the head. There is a lot of confusion. There is a lot of error. And there's a lot of me-ism involved in what we profess as belief in God.

Somebody in our congregation recently suggested that it might be helpful if I spent a little time talking about the New Age movement because of the incursion of New Age thinking in our educational system and in our business world. Then I remembered something I learned many years ago when I was a young bank examiner. One of the things I was required to do was to look for counterfeit currency.

I remember asking one of the senior inspectors, "How do I discern counterfeit currency? Can you give me some tips?"

He replied, "That won't be necessary."

"Why not?" I said, surprised.

"Because you have spent years of your life counting the real thing. As soon as you touch the counterfeit, you'll recognize it instinctively."

There's a very real sense in which, if we concentrate on the counterfeit, we can become confused. It is possible the best thing we can do is concentrate on the orthodox, on the real thing. And if we concentrate on the real thing, then the counterfeit becomes readily apparent to us.

Our Need for a Creed

What does it really mean to believe Christianity? It's helpful to go back and study one of the ancient creeds of the Christian church, the Apostles' Creed. Now some of you may be thinking, *That's rather strange. Why go to an ancient creed to talk about believing in the modern world?* But let me remind you why the creeds came into being in the first place. The apostles were going around preaching, and a lot of people were being saved out of either Judaism or paganism. Saved, that is, in the sense of finding their salvation in Christ. These early Christians realized rather quickly their basic need for some fundamental statement, some solid basis of teaching in succinct form. Remember, the Bible was not available in those days as it is now. So the creeds were formed to meet this need—to give a powerful statement of orthodox Christian belief.

Another concern that emphasized the need for a unified creed was that the Christian church was being bombarded by all kinds of heretical beliefs. Somebody has pointed out that there are really no new heresies—that they were all dealt with within the first five centuries of the Christian experience. Old heresies simply get re-vamped and come up in new guises, but they are the same old heresies nevertheless. And you'll find that the creeds were often developed as a specific way of addressing the heretical incursions in Christian thinking.

The third reason for the creed was so it could aid Christians in making a clearer statement of their faith, in order that they might confess what they truly believed.

One of the best known creeds is the one commonly called the Apostles' Creed, which has led many people to believe that the apostles put it together. There were various legends about this, and in the early days of the church there were those who believed quite sincerely that that was actually what happened.

Let me give you an example of a sermon based on this assumption. This is probably from the eighth century:

On the tenth day after the Ascension, the disciples composed the creed. Peter said, "I believe in God the Father Almighty, maker of heaven and earth."

And Andrew said, "and in Jesus Christ his only Son our Lord."

James added, "suffered under Pontius Pilate, was crucified, dead and buried."

And Thomas said, "He descended into hell and on the third day rose again from the dead."

And James said, "And he ascended into heaven, and sits on the right hand of the Father Almighty."

And Philip added, "Thence he will come to judge the living and the dead."

Bartholemew said, "I believe in the Holy Spirit."

And Matthew added, "the holy catholic church, the communion of saints."

And Simon said, "the remission of sins."

And Thaddeus, "the resurrection of the flesh."

And Matthias concluded, "with the life everlasting."

This is somewhat fanciful, but it is nice to think there was a time when all the apostles agreed on something. Therefore, we will turn to the Apostles' Creed and look at it from this point of view. The word *creed* comes from the Latin *credo,* which literally means "I believe." What you believe does matter. Belief is genuinely important.

Making sense of our experiences

Psychologists have some interesting observations about and insights into belief. This is what they tell us: that in our lives we are subjected to all kinds of experiences, and we have an innate desire to make sense out of these experiences. Accordingly, we build a system of belief to help explain the experiences to which we're subjected.

So, for instance, if a tragedy happens, and somebody close to me goes down in an airplane crash, it's traumatic; it's difficult for me to handle. How do I cope with it? Probably by establishing a system of belief concerning that particular event. So I may say, "I believe that God is sovereign. I believe that God created my loved one. I believe there is a time to be born and a time to die. I believe that none of us dies before his time, that there are no accidents with God, and that God has called my loved one home." I would bring a system of belief into the handling of an experience.

On the other hand, it is quite possible that I would react by saying, "How can you say there is an almighty God if something like that happens? If God was almighty, there is no way he would have let that happen. And how can you say that this almighty God is loving? If he was loving, he would not have taken this loved one away from me!" And so, I will decide at that particular time to believe that God almighty, who is loving, cannot possibly exist. That's how I would make sense of that experience.

The influence of subcultures

Another factor that psychologists point out to us is that we all absorb ideas from our subcultures. If I was brought up in a God-fearing, Christian home, if I was well-taught in Christian theology, then it is highly probable that I would respond to that particular situation by saying that God is sovereign, that he created us, that there is a time to be born and a time to die, and that God's will should be done. I might say, "The Lord has given, the Lord has taken away, blessed be the name of the Lord." Having absorbed my ideas from a Christian subculture, I would now use those ideas to make sense out of my experience.

If, on the other hand, I was brought up the way well-known atheist Bertrand Russell was brought up, my reaction would almost

5

certainly be different. Bertrand Russell's father left word in his will that his son was to be raised as an atheist. If I was raised in that kind of subculture, then it would not be surprising if I would make sense out of these circumstances by absorbing the ideas of my subculture and applying them to this situation.

The result of all this is that a person discovers some degree of security in their situation. In other words, if I am confronted with this traumatic accident, but I have absorbed from my Christian subculture concepts about the sovereignty and the grace and love of God, I will find great comfort in those concepts. I will honestly, genuinely believe that God has taken my loved one to himself. On the other hand, if I was raised in an atheistic subculture, where I absorbed atheistic ideas, I will find comfort in the fact that their time on earth is up, and they simply do not exist anymore. I would not need to worry about them anymore. I might think, *It was great while they were here, and there were many happy memories, but now I need to get on with living.*

Psychologists are very helpful in analyzing how we as human beings work, yet I think often they do not go far enough. Blaise Pascal wrote in his *Penseés,*

There are three sources of belief: reason, custom, and inspiration. The mind must be open to proofs, must be confirmed by custom, and offer itself in humbleness to inspirations which alone can produce a true and saving effect.

I think Pascal is saying basically that reason equates to what the psychologists call "making sense out of experience" and custom equates to "absorbing ideas from subcultures." But he adds the third very important point that psychologists often overlook. It is what Pascal calls "inspiration." By that he means that we have to factor in God intervening in human affairs and bringing to our understanding things that are beyond our experience.

We all believe

When we put these three things together—reason, custom, and inspiration—we can begin to understand how we function as "believers." Everyone you have ever met is a "believer," for there is no way you can function in society except by believing. We are extremely fragile pieces of creation. We are utterly dependent, and dependence is a part of belief. We are very limited in our finite intellectual capabilities. There is so much that we have to take by faith, and often we do not have empirical evidence upon which to base our beliefs.

There is no way we can cope with the vastness of experience without some degree of faith. Living in society requires an element of trust: When you put your money in a bank or when you sign any kind of contract, there is an element of trust. When you marry someone, there is an element of trust. You cannot function without it. And so everybody is a believer in something. The question, however, is, "What is the belief in, how real is it, and how consistently is it being applied?"

Why Is Belief Important?

Hebrews 11:6 says, "Anyone who comes to him must believe that he exists and that he rewards those who earnestly seek him." You either believe that God is, or you believe that God is not. But you are a believer either way.

It is not possible to categorically prove or disprove the existence of God on the basis of purely empirical evidence. When a person comes to an understanding or experience of the reality of the existence of God, an element of faith inevitably has to come into it. If I believe that God is, as opposed to believing that God is not, that is going to affect the whole course of my life. Immediately I have parted company with my neighbor if I believe that God is and they believe that God is not. The rest of our lives are going to be different from that moment on.

Hebrews 11:3 says, "By faith we understand that the universe was formed at God's command." There are various theories about our universe. One theory is that it was created by God's almighty word, that he called and brought it into existence. Another theory is that it simply happened. Another theory is that it is infinite; it is without beginning and without end. All of these are beliefs. If I believe that God is, and I believe that the God who is created the universe, then that will affect all my attitudes toward possessions, toward everything material, and toward my existence as a person. If I believe otherwise, then I will think totally differently.

Belief is of phenomenal significance, especially when we get into the spiritual aspect of our lives. By that I mean getting beyond whether God exists or whether the universe was created and beginning to talk about our personal relationship with this God. Scripture says, "For it is by grace you have been saved, through faith" (Ephesians 2:8). Not only do I believe that God exists and that he created the universe, but I also believe that this same God has reached out in love and grace toward me, and that by faith I have received from him salvation through Christ. However, if I believe that God is not, or if I believe that he has not created the world and that salvation is entirely up to me (there is no such thing as a free lunch, and what you get in this life depends on what you do), then clearly, my approach to life will be totally different from the approach of the person who believes that he has been saved by grace through faith.

We live by what we believe

Hebrews goes on to say that those who have been saved, that is, the righteous, will live by faith. Now there are various ways of living. Some people live on the basis of "unless I see it, I won't believe it." Actually, that is not how they really work, but that is what they profess. They operate on the basis of empirical evidence. They insist that nothing is real if they cannot experience it through their senses of touch, taste, sight, etc. And that if they cannot rationalize this thing then it does not exist. People who live this way do not live by faith. People who live by faith, however, are those who believe that God is, that he created the universe, that he reaches out in love and grace and allows them by faith to know him. People who live by faith believe that this same God is intimately concerned in all the affairs of human life, and they live a life of dependence upon him. And so you see, whether I believe that I live by faith or not, belief is going to determine how I live my life.

By faith we stand

In 2 Corinthians 5:7 we are told that "We live by faith, not by sight." We're also told in 2 Corinthians 1:24 that "It is by faith you stand firm." When we are going through life's experiences, many things prove difficult for us. Sometimes we have a tendency to be bowled over by them. The big question is: How can I cope with life? How can I stand under all these overwhelming circumstances? Well, the answer in Scripture is *by faith we stand*. In other words, as the overwhelming circumstances of life come over me, I can either find strength in the God who created the universe, who in love and grace has reached out to me and saved me, or I simply stand on my own two feet and say, "You've got to hack it out for yourself, and that's all there is to life." And if I choose the pull-myself-up-by-my-own-bootstraps approach, I'm going to be a very different person from the person who stands by faith. "This is the victory," Scripture says, "even our faith." Some people say, "This is the victory, doing the best you can." And so our lives are lived according to the beliefs that we have.

The ingredients of belief

Today when we talk about *belief* we don't always mean what the Scriptures mean by *belief*. When you find *belief* or *faith* in the Bible, you'll always find key little words with them like *hotē*,

9

which basically means, "I believe *that* something is true or some-one is trustworthy." Now that's where belief begins. I believe on the basis of some proposition that the proposition is true.

Let's look at an example. Someone tells me one day that London is in England: I believe that London is in England. Somebody tells me that 2 + 2 = 4: I believe that 2 + 2 = 4. Basically, this is a proposition: I believe that it is true. Often you'll find, however, that that is as far as belief goes when it comes to religious experience. But if you look carefully in Scripture, you'll find that Scripture starts with believe *hoté*.

That's only the beginning. You then need to look at what the Bible means when it talks about belief and belief *epi*. The idea here is that my belief that something is true, or that someone is trustwor-thy, now requires me to rely upon that thing or that person that I believe is true or trustworthy. For instance, say I believe that air-planes fly from Milwaukee to New York. I have a daughter and son-in-law in New York. I believe that airplanes flying to New York, if I got on them, would take me to New York. I believe that all these propositions are true. But believing that all these things are true never gets me any nearer New York. I have to believe *into*. I have to believe *upon*. I have to believe *epi*. I've already believed that it is true, and now my belief moves out of the realm of the intellectual into the realm of actual reliance.

Third, as I get on that plane, I fasten my seat belt and I relax and *lay hold of*, or *lean upon* or *draw from*, all the unique resources of the airplane. In actual fact, the law of aerodynamics now takes over the law of gravity, and I fly. I am now believing *eis*. I am laying hold of something, leaning upon it, drawing resources from it.

When we talk about belief in the Bible, we're not just saying that we believe that God exists. That's where we start, but we go further than that. I believe that God exists. I believe that, because he is God, he is reliable and trustworthy, and because I believe that he is trustworthy, I will rely upon him. In doing so I will draw from him the resources needed to live life as I was intended to live it. I begin to believe.

Sir Kenneth Clark, who produced "Civilization," one of the most popular television series of all time, said this in his autobiography:

> I had a religious experience. It took place in the church of San Lorenzo but did not seem to be connected with the harmonious beauty of the architecture. I could only say that for a few minutes my whole being was irradiated by a kind of heavenly joy far more intense than anything I had known before. This state of mind lasted for several minutes and, wonderful though it was, posed an awkward problem in terms of action. My life was far from blameless; I would have to reform. My family would think I was going mad. And perhaps after all it was a delusion, for I was in every way unworthy of receiving such a flood of grace. Gradually the effect wore off, and I made no effort to retain it. I think I was right. I was too deeply embedded in the world to change course.

Quite a testimony from Sir Kenneth, now Lord Clark! Notice, if you will, that he presumably had been part of a subculture of belief at some time. Brought up in England, he probably had been packed off to an English public school where he had mandatory chapel in the Anglican church every morning. So he would have learned the creeds, the collects, the readings, and the Scriptures. He had imbibed some teaching so that when he had an experience that he called an "irradiation by a kind of heavenly joy," he immediately identified this as a flood of grace. Isn't that interesting? He also recognized that if this grace flooding his soul was to be acted upon (notice the word *acted),* it would be necessary for him "to reform." Yet he knew that if he were to reform, people would think he was crazy, and he wasn't sure if he might be crazy, and, anyway, he was too deeply embedded in his world. So he let it pass and did nothing about it.

He believed that he was experiencing joy. He believed that it had to do with grace. He believed that it required action. He believed all these things, but he did not believe *into* them. He did not rely upon them. He did not draw resources from them. He was, by the biblical definition, not believing.

Believing in God As Person

William Law says, in marked contrast, "If you have not chosen God, it will make no difference in the end what you have chosen. For you have missed the purpose for which you were formed, and you will have forsaken the only thing that satisfies." In other words, if you believe that God is, that he reaches out to you in grace and offers you all that is needed for life and for eternity— if you believe it is true but never come to the point of action in terms of commitment, then it doesn't matter what else you choose in life. You didn't choose correctly from the beginning, so William Law says.

Confidence in a person

In Romans chapter 4, Paul brings out four simple propositions concerning Abraham's faith. The first one is this, that Abraham's faith was confidence in a person. Verse 17 talks about God, in whom he, that is, Abraham, believed—"The God who gives life to the dead and calls things that are not as though they were."

The thing that determines the validity of our faith is its object. I can get on a plane at Milwaukee Airport, planning to see my daughter and son-in-law, and when the thing takes off, a woman may ask, "And who are you going to visit in the Twin Cities today?"

And I say, "I'm not going to the Twin Cities; I'm going to New York."

And she responds, "This is the Minneapolis flight."

I say, "I believe it's going to New York." I can have intense belief in error if I wish, but it will not result in truth. It will not result in reality. The plane is still flying to Minneapolis no matter how hard I believe it is going to New York!

During wintertime in Milwaukee it's clear that some people exercise phenomenal faith. They believe that water, when it is frozen, turns into ice. They believe that ice, when it is thick enough, will bear their weight, so they drive their cars, their dog sleds, and their snowmobiles on it and drown by faith. Nothing, absolutely nothing, is wrong with their faith at all, but the object of their faith is totally unworthy of such faith. Conversely and ironically, very minimal faith in very thick ice will keep you as secure as if you're standing on reinforced concrete. It is not the volume of your faith that's primarily important; it's the object.

Whom did Abraham believe? He believed God, and he believed two things about him: number one, that he brings life out of deadness, and number two, that he speaks the word and things that did not exist come into existence. And Abraham had absolute confidence in this God. And that was the essence of his faith: confidence in a person.

Awareness of the problems

There are those who decry faith because they think that people who believe are simple obscurantists; that is, that they are simply people who close their eyes to realities. They are the sort of people who say, "My mind is made up; please do not confuse it with facts." They have decided what they are going to believe, and that's how it is. I don't think I ever met a person who didn't operate on that basis in one form or another. However, true faith in the biblical sense is not obscurantist. It does not close its eyes to reality. It does not check its mind in the church cloakroom. True faith is prepared to be fully conversant with the problems.

Notice what it says about Abraham in verse 19: "Without weakening in his faith, he faced the fact that his body was as good as dead—since he was about a hundred years old—and that Sarah's womb was also dead." Abraham faced two facts. Number one, he was about a hundred years old, and therefore, as far as reproduction was concerned, his chances were slightly less than zilch. Number two, his wife couldn't have children when she was young; she was

pushing a hundred now herself, and so the chances of her repro-
ducing are equally slightly less than zilch. However, God stuck
out his divine neck and said, "Abraham, you're going to have a
son, and as a result of that son, you will become the father of
many nations."

Suddenly Abraham has to square his confidence in a person with
the fact that he is conversant with the problems. What does he do?
He carefully evaluates the problems and he thinks to himself, *My
first problem is this: My body is as good as dead, but I believe in
God, and one of the things I believe about him is that he brings life
out of deadness.* Slowly a smile crosses his hundred-year-old face,
and he says to himself, *My problem is really a divine opportunity.
For if my body is as good as dead, and God says he's going to bring
life out of deadness, that will prove conclusively that he is the God
who brings life out of deadness.*

Very happy with this, he then faces his second problem: He goes
to see his wife. I've often wondered if he said, "Honey, you're
going to get pregnant." I'd love to have been a fly on the tent wall
at that particular time. We don't know how he broached the subject.
We do know that she went mildly hysterical and just about died
laughing, which is understandable. We also know that she came to
believe in the end, and we know how she did it. For she confronted
the fact, and the fact was that her womb had a nonexistent capacity
to reproduce. But Abraham reminded her about the God in whom
they believed. And one of the things they believed about God was
this: He had the ability to bring out of nonexistent capacity things
that did not exist. Therefore, her problem was an opportunity in
exactly the same way that his problem was an opportunity. And,
fully conversant with the facts, they were totally confident in the
person. That is faith.

Perseverance

The third proposition about Abraham's faith is that it was consistent
in its progress. There were many delays, disappointments, and

14

wrong turns. But the Scriptures tell us, in verse 20, "He did not waver through unbelief regarding the promise of God, but was strengthened in his faith and gave glory to God."

F. B. Meyer says, "So often we mistake God and interpret his delays as denials." Saint Gregory said, "All holy desires heighten in intensity with the delay of fulfillment, and desire which fades with delay was never holy desire at all." As far as Abraham was concerned, the delays and the disappointments served only to strengthen his faith.

The Korean Christians, suffering terribly under the communist insurgence, had a motto: "We are like nails. The harder you hit us, the deeper you drive us." That's faith responding to the divine delays and divine disappointments by being strengthened because it is focused in a deep confidence in God.

Being convinced of God's promises

Verse 21 says, "being fully persuaded that God had power to do what he had promised." When I was a young evangelist with a wife and three small children living in England, my wife occasionally said to me after I'd been gone for months on end, "You need a vacation; you need time off with your children." I never had time to do it. I never did it.

But on one occasion, just to stop her reminding me of this, I said, "Okay, I'll take you to the Mediterranean; we'll sit in the sunshine, the beautiful white sand, the gorgeous blue sea." You've got to understand that for people living in Britain, the Mediterranean is heaven.

Her response to this promise of mine was, "That's not funny, Stuart; I don't like you talking like that." The reason she responded like that was this: When I promised, she knew I didn't mean it. If I meant it, she knew I couldn't afford it. If I could have afforded it, she knew that I would not have made it a priority. And, therefore, the possibilities were nil. So she didn't take a promise like that seriously at all.

15

Round about that time, I got a phone call from a friend of mine, Norman Whiteley. Norman Whiteley was a very successful businessman, a real rascal of a fellow, who didn't believe that I, his banker, preached in my spare time. And when I told him I did, he said, "I just don't believe it."

I said, "Okay, I'll be preaching at a certain church tonight; you come and find out." He hadn't been to a church in his life before. He came late, walked right down to the front, put his feet upon the pulpit, crossed his arms, and grinned at me the whole way through. He got converted that night.

Norman was a very generous man. Norman had chartered an aircraft, filled it with senior citizens, rented the top floor of a motel in Mallorca in the Mediterranean, and given all those senior citizens a week's vacation at his expense. That was the kind of guy Norman was. He called me one day, and this is what he said: "The first two weeks of August I booked a flight to Mallorca and back for you and Jill and the three kids. I've made reservations in a hotel for you. You're going at my expense. This is to say thank you for all that you've done in my life and to tell you I love you. And to make sure you go, my wife and I are coming with you."

I put the phone down, and I turned around and Jill said, "What was that?"

I said, "I was just finalizing details of our trip to the Mediterranean."

She said, "Listen, I don't want you joking about this anymore. I feel very strongly about it; you need a vacation. You should have time with the children. And I don't want you talking like this anymore. It's just not fair."

I said, "Norman said so." And her attitude changed completely—because when I said it, I didn't mean it. But when Norman said it, she knew he meant it. She also knew he had the resources to do it. And she also knew if Norman said he would do it, he would come through. So she turned to the kids and said, "Kids, let's pack. We're going to the Mediterranean." That's faith.

Now there are people who say they believe in God and never go to church, who never show outwardly that they have a genuine commitment to Christ and his church. If they do go to church, it is not because they believe it is the repository of truth or the basis of moral authority. They go in order that they might get spiritual strokes. Sorry, folks—that isn't good enough. What we believe and how we believe *totally* affects the people we are. And in this modern society, there's so much confusion that we need to clarify what we believe. I trust that this book will help.

MAKING IT PRACTICAL

1. What were the three reasons the creeds came into being? Why is it helpful to study the ancient creeds today?

2. What did Pascal say are the three sources of belief? How have these three affected what you believe?

3. What are some beliefs, commonly held among evangelical Christians, that may need to be examined in light of Scripture?

4. How might we be guilty of creating and listening to "gods of our own imagination," or attributing our own thoughts and feelings to God? How can we be sure we are believing in and listening to the one true God revealed in Scripture?

5. Looking back on the past few years, think of one instance where your beliefs impacted your response to or handling of a tragedy or difficult situation. What did you learn about what you truly believed?

2

"I Believe in God the Father Almighty"

Exodus 33:12-16; 34:6-8

The results of a youth survey taken in Canada reveal a number of striking things. For instance, I was surprised to notice that 84 percent of the young people said they believed in God. However, only 10 percent said that God had "a great deal" of influence on how they lived. More than 80 percent of them said they wanted religious weddings and funerals, but less than half of 1 percent said that they would seek any religious counsel or instruction.

"Belief in God" carries diverse meanings

I think Edmund Burke had a point when he said that man "by his constitution is a religious animal." I think what he meant was this: There is something inherently religious about humanity; we always look for something or someone bigger or grander than ourselves upon which to rely, to whom we give our worship. However, if it is true that, for instance, in Canada, 84 percent of the young people believe in God but have no practical application of that belief, I think it's rather obvious that the god of many people's religion needs some clarification.

Ayn Rand, a Russian who came over to the United States and wrote a number of novels, was very much opposed to collectivism and very much committed to the freedom of the individual. This is one thing that she wrote: "I am done with the monster of we, the word of serfdom, of plunder, of misery, falsehood and shame. And now I see the free face of God and I raise this God over all the earth, this God who men have sought since men came into being, the God who will grant them joy and peace and pride. This God, this one word, *I*." If you were to ask Ayn Rand, "Do you believe in God?" she probably would have said yes. If you asked her, "Who is this God?" then she most likely would have said, "This God is one word, *I*."

Shirley MacLaine, the Oscar-winning actress, dancer, novelist, and autobiographical writer, has a somewhat different approach. In one of her books, *Out on a Limb,* she tells us, "Not that I am God, but that we are god, that all is god, that we're all part of a cosmic oneness. And if we don't feel that we're god, that's simply because we're ignorant. And the only way that we can banish our ignorance and discover our godness is by enlightenment that will come through meditation." This is Hinduism dressed up in New Ageism.

In addition to telling us that we are gods, she tells us that we have lived before and we'll live again, that there is no such thing as death, and that we have the ability to create our own reality. I suppose, strictly speaking, if you asked Shirley MacLaine, "Do you believe in God?" she would say, emphatically, yes! She would have no difficulty at all standing up and reciting the first four words of the Apostles' Creed, "I believe in God." It's not the God of Ayn Rand; that is "I." The God of Shirley MacLaine is "we." Sandwiched somewhere in between is a more common god, I think, that many people believe in emphatically. Many people have their own god, who is very indulgent, rather weak, near at hand when we want anything, but far away and out of sight when we have a mind to do wrong. Such a god is as much an idol as if he were an image of stone.

"I believe in God" could mean "I am god." "I believe in God" could mean, "we are god." "I believe in God" could mean, "I believe in a very indulgent, rather weak god who's near at hand when I can use him and is conveniently absent when he's an embarrassment to me." We can say, "I believe in God," but what do we mean when we affirm the Apostles' Creed, "I believe in God the Father Almighty?"

Belief in God

As I pointed out in the previous chapter, we start believing when we come to an intelligent conclusion that something is true. We believe in God when we come to conclusions about God. How do we arrive at these conclusions about God? For instance, how do we arrive at conclusions concerning God's existence, his nature, attributes, and purposes? Well, we start out discovering reality, coming to conclusions through reason and through revelation. These are the two main avenues that allow us to come to conclusions about God. Down through the centuries there have been several arguments from rationality concerning the existence of God. Three of these have rather long words that are rather overpowering. The words are *ontological, cosmological,* and *teleological,* but you'll notice that they're all logical!

Arguments from reason

The ontological argument was developed by Archbishop Anselm many centuries ago. He says that people somehow or other have a concept of God as "a being, than which nothing greater can be conceived." His argument, very much simplified, is basically this: If man has the ability to conceive of something greater than which can be conceived, then there must be reality behind this human conception. Although many have argued against the ontological argument, it still raises a point worth considering.

The cosmological argument comes from Aquinas. He argues from contingency or from what he believes is the principle of cause and effect. The things that we see happen have a reason for happening. If suddenly a brick comes whistling through the air in my

21

direction while I am preaching, it is possible that there will be two reactions: number one, I will duck; and number two, we will look around to see who threw it. Now why should we assume somebody threw it? Why can't we just assume the brick took it into its brick-ish head to hurtle itself in my direction, perhaps feeling that what I was saying was anti-brick? We would not assume that. We would assume every effect, that is, a brick hurtling through the air, has a cause. Cause and effect.

If we argue backwards, then eventually we have to ask the question, Is there a first cause? Is there something that initially caused something, of which we see the effects all around us? They didn't just happen; There was a reason behind them. We then ask the question, Was there an unmoved mover? Is there an uncaused cause? And the answer probably would be yes. It is either an infinite universe that was uncaused and is unchanging, or an infinite God who was uncaused and is unchanging. It seems from the argument that we back up to an infinite universe or an infinite God.

The problem with the infinite universe argument is, among other things, the second law of thermodynamics. The second law of thermodynamics teaches us that there are hot things and cold things, and if you put a hot thing next to a cold thing, the hot thing will cool and the cool thing will warm, because the energy of heat will flow from one to the other. And in the end, the hot will have cooled and the cooled will have heated until they are the same temperature, and then you have non-energy; you have entropy. Our universe is cooling down. If it's cooling down, that suggests that at one stage, it will end. If it has an end, it is reasonable to assume it has a beginning. Therefore, the universe is not infinite, which leaves us with a conclusion that the uncaused cause, the unmoved mover, is not an infinite universe but an infinite God. That is basically the cosmological argument.

Voltaire put the teleological argument rather simply: "If a watch proves the existence of a watchmaker, but the universe does not prove the existence of a great architect, then I consent to be called a fool." To put it positively, what he is saying is this: If it is reasonable to assume that the intricate design of a watch presumes the existence of a watch designer, it is equally reasonable to assume that the intricacies of the universe presuppose an intelligent designer of the universe. It would be utterly nonsensical to suggest that a watch could create itself. It would be even more nonsensical to suggest that the universe could do the same. The teleological argument is an argument from design.

Another traditional argument for the existence of God is the moral argument. Man has a sense of morality. He has a sense of fair and unfair, ought and ought not, should and should not. Where in the world did he get this moral sensitivity? The answer from the moral argument is that there is a source of morality, justice, and righteousness, and that source we call God. People object to that sometimes. They'll say, "People learn their morality from their surroundings, from their society." The problem is that some of the most moral people that we acclaim, we acclaim because they stood out against the prevailing morality of their society. And rather than being the products of it, they have been the changers of it. The moral argument, then, is that man's sense of morality presupposes an ultimate morality. These are some of the arguments from reason for the existence of God, and they should be understood and carefully considered.

Even if you agree with all those arguments for God's existence, you don't necessarily finish up with the God of the Bible. There are still great holes in your understanding of God. You don't finish up with God the Father of our Lord Jesus Christ. You need revelation in addition to reason. However, many people are not prepared to accept revelation; we must start with them on the basis of reason. And Paul seemed to be open to doing this as well. Writing to the Romans, Paul pointed out to them that the invisible things of God are clearly seen in the things that are created. In other words, he would argue from creation to the existence of God. And the psalmist seems to do the same thing when he reminds us that the heavens declare the glory of God. The earth and firmament show forth his handiwork, arguing from the universe to the existence, the nature, and the attributes of God.

I like what Pascal said. He had what he called his famous wager, and this is how it went: If I believe in God and then die and I'm wrong, I've lost nothing. But if you believe that God does not exist, and then you die and find you were wrong, you've lost everything. Pascal said that, with those kind of options, you wager on the existence of God. That is the minimum level at which some people can begin to approach the possibility of God's existence.

Arguments from revelation

In addition to reason, we need to look at revelation as well. In Exodus 33:12–34:8, Moses is having an encounter with God. And here God tells him, "I will cause all my goodness to pass in front of you, and I will proclaim my name, the LORD, in your presence." God is prepared to take the initiative and reveal to us things concerning himself that we could never rationalize on our own because we have finite intellectual capabilities, and these capabilities are utterly incapable of comprehending the infinite.

You can't get the ocean in a thimble. You can put the thimble in the ocean and get enough ocean in the thimble to understand the characteristics of the ocean, but there's no way you can include the whole ocean in a thimble. Finite minds cannot comprehend an infinite God. But if an infinite God pours his ocean-ness into our thimble-ness, then we can understand something of who he is by revelation, still recognizing finitely we can never understand his infinite being. And that's what Scripture is all about. Scripture is the infinite God revealing himself to finite people, taking the initiative and pouring his ocean-ness into our thimble-ness in order that we might grasp something of who he is that we could never understand without his revelation. If, therefore, we're to have solid Christian belief in God, we utilize reason and revelation. And then we can speak with compelling effect to our modern world. Could you say, "I believe in God?" If so, you would presume that your answer would be open to the question why. And presumably, if you affirm that you believe in God, then you would be open to answer the question, "What's he like? Tell me about him." That's what Christian belief and the modern world is all about. We arrive at conclusions concerning him. But there's a lot more to believing in God than just arriving at a conclusion.

From conclusions to confidence

The second aspect of belief is that we then place our confidence in him. This is illustrated for us in the encounter between Moses and God. You'll notice that Moses talks to God about the tasks that God has given him. And he says that he really is not at all excited about doing it unless he has some assurance of God's presence. God responds by saying, "My presence will go with you." And Moses seems to be well satisfied with this. And now we see him moving from a conclusion about God to confidence in him.

"If you're going with me," says Moses, "I'll go. If you won't go with me, forget it, with all due respect." He is expressing his confidence in the God about whom he's arrived at a conclusion. Clearly, this is an aspect of belief in God. But we go a step further. To believe in God means I develop a relationship with him or I converse with him. This is illustrated for us again in this passage, for Moses says to God, "Teach me your ways so that I may know you." And then he talks about this continuing in order that he might continue to find favor with God. To believe in God starts with conclusions about him, develops into confidence in him, and then matures into a conversation with him. I begin to learn of him. I begin to discover more about him. I increase in the knowledge of God. And as I do, it begins to demonstrate itself in the person that I am and the life that I live.

Moses said, "The only reason that anybody is going to believe that we are special people is if there's clear evidence that you are with us. Our confidence is in you, we trust you implicitly, we need to know you more thoroughly, we encourage and are committed to an ongoing relationship with you." This is what it means to believe in God. And all this is summarized in commitment to him. Conclusions about him, confidence in him, conversation with him, commitment to him. After there is conversation and God's revelation of his character to Moses, Moses responds by bowing to the ground at once and worshipping. And that, of course, is the appropriate posture of those who profess to believe in God.

Confucius said, "The essence of knowledge is having it to apply it." If I have come to the knowledge of God, the essence of that knowledge is applying it in terms of commitment to him, confidence in him, and conversation with him.

Belief in God the Father

If belief in God gives us the sense of authority because of who he is, belief in God the Father is intended to give us a sense of affiliation, of intimacy. Two aspects of God are revealed in Scripture. One, he is transcendent. He is high and holy and reigns and rules separate from us. And the other aspect, the balancing aspect, is that he is immanent. He is close and intimate, and we can know him personally. So when we say, "I believe in God," we can be talking about his transcendence. When we talk about belief in God the Father, we're introduced to the concept of his immanence. We have affinity with him.

In the Old Testament, there are not many references to God as Father. When you find them, they usually refer to him as creator. Pointing out the fact that we're all created by him and, therefore, in that limited sense, we're all the children of God, Malachi, for instance, says, "Have we not all one father?" Paul, debating with the philosophers in Athens, quoted one of the Athenian poets. And he said, "We are all his offspring." Apparently he quoted it with approval, pointing out again this idea that the Father as creator has brought us into being. However, Malachi does point out this question on God's behalf, where he says, "If I am a Father, where is the honor due to me?" If we believe in God the Father as creator, it is reasonable for him to ask, "If you say I'm your Father, where is the honor due to me?" It's a good question, and one that we ought to answer.

Some people therefore have the idea that because the Bible speaks of God as the Father of us all, everybody is going to finish up in heaven. They begin with "God the Father" and finish with universalism. It's interesting and important to notice that both of these passages, in Malachi and Acts, also talk about divine judgment and point out that there are those who will not come into blessing but will come under his judgment. And so even these statements that talk about him being Father of all do not allow for universalism.

In the Old Testament "God the Father" is related to his identity as creator, but when we move into the New Testament, the idea of God being Father is related to the Lord Jesus. The Lord Jesus, about a hundred times in John's gospel alone, talks about the Father. He used a very interesting word for *Father*. It was the Aramaic word *Abba*. When a little baby starts to stammer something in the English language, one of the first words he will probably say is *Dada*. The Aramaic equivalent of *Dada* is *Abba*. When Jesus began to use this deeply intimate, wonderfully personal word to describe God, he scandalized the people. They were offended that he could talk about God in such an intimate, familiar way. And yet, repeatedly, he did it. He then added to the controversy by saying, "I and the Father are one. The Father is in me and I in the Father." He was speaking of the intimacy, the affinity, that he, as the Son, had with the Father.

In John 20:17, Jesus talked about "my Father" and "your Father." And when the disciples asked how they should pray, he said, "When you pray, 'Our Father . . .'" Clearly Jesus was linking his well-defined sense of intimacy and affinity with the Father with the affinity his disciples would enjoy with God. He was introducing them to a sense of the Father's loving care, intimate interest, and concern.

You'll remember on one occasion he asked these questions: Now if an earthly father would not give his son a snake when he asked for a fish, and if an earthly father would not give his son a stone when he asked for bread, is it not reasonable to assume that your heavenly Father will behave in at least the way an earthly father will, and if you ask him, he will give you what you need? No serpents for fish from God your father. No stones for bread from God your father. Your heavenly Father knows what you need and will provide for you. He was introducing them to this tremendous sense of intimacy and affinity with the Father.

How, you ask, do we become children of the heavenly Father? And the New Testament has two answers to that question for us: Number one, through adoption. Number two, through regeneration. Adoption means that the Sovereign reaches out and chooses us to be his children. I remember on one occasion staying with a delightful family in New England. They had two daughters who didn't look at all alike. One of them looked very much like her father, and the other girl looked totally different. As we were talking, it suddenly dawned on me why the other girl looked so different. And she told me quite openly, "I was adopted. My sister is the natural child of my parents, but I was adopted."

Because we were getting along very well I said, "I've always wanted to ask somebody who's adopted this question: 'Do you feel different from your sister?' "

And she said, "Yes, of course I feel different."

I said, "In what way?"

She said, "Oh, they just had her, but they chose me."

"They just had her, but they chose me." Now there's the emphasis of adoption. When we become children of the Father through adoption, it is because he chose us to be his children.

The other aspect of becoming the children of God, so that we call him Father, is that we have been born again by the Spirit of God. In the same way that the human father transmits life to the children, so our heavenly Father imparts his life to us. And through Christ's ministry to us in the person of the Holy Spirit, we become partakers of the divine nature. We're born again of the Spirit of God.

Accordingly, Paul tells us the Spirit bears witness with our spirit, and we cry "Abba, Father." We are able to relate intimately to this transcendent God. When, therefore, I affirm I believe in God the Father, I ought to be affirming that I've been adopted into his family, that I'm regenerated by the Holy Spirit, that I have an affinity with him, and that he, the great transcendent one, is near and dear, I have access to him, and he hears my every prayer.

If we're talking, however, about Christian belief and the modern world, we need to recognize that not everybody is excited about the doctrine of God as father.

If I were to ask you, "Are you a feminist?" I may get a number of answers from you. But let me point out to you that *feminist,* like many other labels, can mean a lot of different things. "M.A.S.H." star Alan Alda says a feminist is somebody who believes that women are human. J. I. Packer, that most conservative of English theologians, went to a conference on one occasion, wrote about it, and said, "On my way home I discovered to my amazement that I, of all people, am a feminist. For I discovered that a feminist, in the truer sense of the word, is a person that believes that women should be free to enjoy all that God intended them to enjoy." Packer said, "I'm a feminist." So am I. However, there are feminists, and there are radical feminists.

There are also radical Christian feminists. I've spent some time this week reading some of their work. One of the most interesting, erudite, and articulate of these radical Christian feminists is Dr. Rosemary Radford Reuther. I've been reading her books *Women Church* and *Sexism and God Talk.* She is very much opposed to what she sees as patriarchalism in religion. She says it is one of the reasons for the abuse in our world, the male domination, male abuse of female, etc. She believes this abuse stems, directly or indirectly, from the patriarchalism of Scripture, locked up in the concept of God the Father. She says that things have got to change for women in our world. And this is only going to happen when this patriarchalism is put in its proper place, when the idea of God the Father is put on the shelf, and we begin to see God in broader terms. She's opposed, in many ways, to the use of God as Father.

She has written liturgy for women to be used in church. A liturgy, for instance, for women who have been raped, a liturgy for women who had an abortion, a liturgy for the marriage of lesbian lovers—that sort of thing. And the liturgy addresses God as "Father and Mother," or addresses the goddess as the mother of the creator.

This is her reasoning for addressing the mother of the creator: She says that the myth of Jehovah as God the father was relatively recent in the near East religions. Predating this was the myth of the goddess who is the mother of the creator. Dr. Reuther stresses that if we are to get rid of patriarchalism, we've got to reintroduce the worship of the goddess, the mother of the creator. And that our liturgy should begin to reflect this.

This may be totally foreign to the majority of us, but let me just point this out to you: There are many sharp, intelligent, upwardly mobile women in our society today who are totally turned off to the church of Jesus Christ. They are totally opposed to the doctrine of God the Father. We have a responsibility to meet them, to minister to them, to build bridges to them, and to get across to them the great good news of God the Father of our Lord Jesus Christ. How are we going to do it? We will never do it until we understand what we mean by God the Father, until we understand their objections to it, and until we can truly exercise Christian belief in the modern world.

Dr. Carl Henry has a helpful note on this point: "The God of the Bible is a sexless God. When Scripture speaks of God as 'he,' the pronoun is primarily personal and generic rather than masculine and specific. It emphasizes God's personality in contrast to impersonal entities." In other words, Dr. Henry is saying that when the Bible talks about God as "he" it is not saying that God is masculine as opposed to feminine. It is saying that God is personal as opposed to impersonal. He is a he as opposed to an it, not a he as opposed to a she. When the Scriptures talk about God as father, they are talking about God's loving care and his graceful provision for us. We need to bear these things in mind if we're to exercise Christian belief in today's world.

There's another group of people who have problems with God as Father. After each service where I address this topic, people have come to talk to me. They're people who in their childhood have had very difficult experiences with their own earthly fathers. One person said to me some time ago, "If God the father is anything like my old man, I refuse to have anything to do with him; I regard him as obscene." This is a major problem for many people.

If we're going to have Christian belief in our present society, we must recognize that there are possibly hundreds of thousands of people in it who have been abused by their fathers and, as a result, have a warped view of fatherhood. When we talk to them about the fatherhood of God, they take their warped view of their earthly father and blow it up to divine proportions, finishing with a grotesque ogre whom they deeply fear. The effect is the exact opposite of what is intended.

If we are to minister to those people (and we must, for this is the society of which we're a part), if we're to minister to them, we must recognize that not infrequently their antagonism to Christianity and their rejection of the Christian church is not for intellectual reasons: it is for psychological reasons. Os Guiness, in his book *In Two Minds,* says this, "True intellectual doubts need answers. But emotionally rooted doubts answer needs." There are some people who will doubt God and doubt the Christian gospel, not for intellectual reasons, but because the thought of them is too painful for them psychologically.

Belief in God the Father Almighty

The third and final point, belief in God the Father Almighty, gives us a sense of God's ability. If you want to read about the almightiness of God, read Job. You'll find the Hebrew word *shaddai* translated "almighty" repeatedly. If you're in the New Testament, you want to read the book of Revelation. There you'll find the Greek word *pantokrator* repeatedly translated "almighty." But as far as we're concerned, the almightiness of God is something that is intended to give us a great sense of divine encouragement and ability. Psalm 91 says, "He who dwells in the shelter of the Most High will rest in the shadow of the Almighty. I will say of the LORD, 'He is my refuge and my fortress, my God, in whom I trust' " (verses 1-2).

A number of years ago, five young men decided they were going to reach out to a primitive tribe of Indians in Ecuador who had never seen a white man. They had done all the survey work; they had made the initial contacts. They were going to fly in a light aircraft into the jungle and land in the only place available to them, a narrow strip of sand on the edge of the river. Nate Saint, the pilot, said, "If it's soft, our wheels will give in; we'll finish up on our nose or our back with a broken plane and no way out." They knew that these Indians were warlike. They knew their lives were in deep jeopardy. The night before they embarked on their attempt to reach these people, they met together and sang "We Rest on Thee Our Shield and Our Defender," the hymn based on Psalm 91. They read Psalm 91, talking about resting in the shadow of the Almighty.

The next morning they flew out. Soon radio contact was lost with them, and a few days later their bodies were found, filled with spears, floating in the river. Every one of them was martyred for the cause of Christ. They went into that situation confident and as-sured. They went into that time of unprecedented danger under the shadow of the Almighty. You say, "He let them down." He didn't let them down. Their widows are the ones who ought to speak to that. For some of their widows then went in, with the children who'd lost their fathers, and became the means of taking the gospel of Christ to the men who'd murdered their husbands and their fathers. Today there's a flourishing church among those very Indians. Why? Because of some people who believed in God the Father Almighty.

J. I. Packer will have the last word. I quote him:

The truth of God's almightiness in creation, providence, and grace is the basis of all our trust, peace, and joy in God. And the same God of all our hopes of answered prayer, present protection, and final salvation. It means that neither fate, nor the stars, nor blind chance, nor man's folly, nor Satan's malice controls this world. Instead, a morally perfect God runs it, and none can dethrone Him or thwart his purposes of love.

MAKING IT PRACTICAL

1. Describe the teleological, cosmological, ontological, and moral arguments for the existence of God.

2. What was Pascal's wager?

3. What is the prevailing concept of God in our society today? How do we know what kind of a god people believe in?

4. Stuart Briscoe describes belief in God as conclusions about him that are proved by confidence in, conversation with, and commitment to him. To what degree is your belief in God evidenced by these three Cs?

5. What does it mean to you to think of God as your heavenly Father? How has your relationship with your earthly father affected your concept of God as Father?

3

"Maker of Heaven and Earth"

Genesis 1

Genesis 1:1 says, "In the beginning God created the heavens and the earth." You will recognize, of course, that this statement, though simple in the extreme, is profound also. "In the beginning God created the heavens and the earth." What do we mean by "in the beginning?" Scientists talk knowledgeably about time equals zero. But what do we mean by "in the beginning of all things?" That's a hard concept for us even to begin to comprehend.

Let me give you an example. When you're sitting in your church building, you might ask yourself, "What was the beginning of this building?" You say, "I remember. I remember being around when they laid the foundations here." Somebody else says, "That's nothing, I came to the groundbreaking." Somebody else says, "That's nothing; I was on the committee that decided we would buy this property." Somebody else says, "That's nothing; I was a member of the church that appointed the committee." And we could go on and on and on.

Whenever the beginning of all things was, God already had been. You'll notice that this verse is not talking about creation. It doesn't say, "In the beginning was the creation." It says, "In the beginning God created . . ." The focus immediately is on the maker of heaven and earth. That's where Scripture starts; that's where it ends; that's what Scripture is all about. If we're to understand Scripture, we're to understand that it is about God the Father Almighty, maker of heaven and earth, and his character, his attributes, his purposes, his power, his expectations, and what he proposes. These are of the utmost significance.

Context makes all the difference

I like the story of the old man in the deep South who was walking along a country road with his dog and his mule. A pickup truck came around the corner too fast and knocked the old man, his dog, and his mule into the ditch. Some time later, there was a court case where the old man claimed damages from the driver of the pickup truck. The counsel for the defense was cross-examining the old man and said, "Answer yes or no to this question. Did you tell the defendant that you were okay?"

The old man answered, "My dog and my mule and me were coming . . ."

He said, "Answer the question, yes or no. Did you tell the defendant you were okay?"

"Me and my dog and my mule . . ."

He said, "Answer the question, yes or no! Did you tell the defendant you were okay?"

He said, "Me and my . . ."

The counsel for the defense interrupted, turned to the judge, and said, "Your honor, would you kindly instruct him to answer the question yes or no."

The judge said, "Let the man say what he is trying to say."

The old man said, "Me and my dog and my mule were coming 'round the bend, and this truck came around too fast and knocked us all into the ditch. And this man here jumped out of the cab. He had a gun, and he went to my dog. It was injured, so he shot it. And he went to the mule and saw that it had a broken leg, so he shot it. And he came and stood over me and said, 'How are you?' And I said, 'I never felt better in my life!' "

Context makes all the difference. It is absolutely true that the man had said to the defendant, "I never felt better in my life." But when you put it into context, you see the true story. If we are to understand Scripture, we recognize it is in the context that in the beginning God created the heavens and the earth. And our focus is on the maker. Of course, our interest automatically goes to what he has made; that is the secondary focus. We start by focusing on the maker.

The Pre-existence of God

We read in Genesis 1:1, "In the beginning God created . . . ." This automatically reminds us of his pre-existence. Scriptures also tell us that in the beginning was the Word, and (the literal tense here) the Word *had already been* in the beginning with God: there was a pre-existence of God.

When we think in terms of the beginning of all things, we come up with a quandary. Some people scoff at the idea that God created the world, as the theologians put it, *ex nihilo*—"out of nothing." They say, "How could God create something out of nothing?" What's the alternative? The alternative, is presumably, that nothing created something out of nothing. Which do you find harder to believe, that nothing created something out of nothing, or that someone created something out of nothing? The biblical statement is abundantly clear. In the beginning God had already been, and he is the creative one, the one in whom all meaning and all reason is to be found; he is pre-existent.

In one of the famous little hymns recorded in the book of Revelation the people around the throne of God sing "he is worthy." And one of the reasons that he is worthy is that he has created all things by his will. This reminds us of his prerogative. Why do things exist that exist? The biblical answer is that they exist because the pre-existent God determined it was his prerogative to bring into being things that did not exist. You've heard the question, Where does a five-hundred-pound gorilla sleep at night? And the answer is, Anywhere he wishes. That is certainly true of five-hundred-pound gorillas, and how much more true of the pre-existent God! He does exactly what he wishes. And if we are to believe the biblical revelation, we accept the fact that before anything was, he was in the state of continuous existence, entire and complete in himself, and he freely chose of his own will to create all things. It was his prerogative, his power.

Hebrews 11:3 reminds us that by faith we understand that the universe was created by the word of God. You remember in Genesis chapter 1, stated over and over again, the expression that God said, "Let there be . . ." and there was. This is strange; this is mysterious. But what it is conveying to us is that God has in himself the power to create, and this power is released in his creative dynamic command: "Let there be . . ." and there was.

When we look in John's gospel, we see the Lord Jesus is described as the Word. When we put the idea of God saying, "Let there be . . ." and there was, together with the idea of Christ being the Word, we understand that things were created by the command of the Word of God, and that there's power in the command of God that enables things to exist. There was a purpose behind it all, too. And the Scriptures tell us that God's purpose in his choice to powerfully create that which did not exist was that he might bring together all things unto one head, even Christ.

We're basically familiar with these things, so when we say, "I believe in God the Father Almighty, maker of heaven and earth," minimally we're speaking of one whose pre-existence, whose prerogative, whose power, and whose purpose we not only understand, but with which we thoroughly agree. Seems pretty simple, doesn't it? However, it gets more complicated when we take those beliefs into today's world.

Making Science God

Is the modern world enthusiastically endorsing this article of the faith? Well, there are many people in the United States of America today who are certainly saying, "I believe in God." But are they believing in this God who is the maker of heaven and earth? That is problematic because faith in what the Bible has to say about God as the maker of all things has been considerably undermined in many segments of our society. People have become very scientific or pseudoscientific in their outlook when they look at what Scripture says. And as a result of that, when they have found a conflict or a presumed conflict between the scientific statement and the spiritual or scriptural revelation, the immediate response has been to discard what the biblical revelation says and to enthrone science as king.

One of the things we have to recognize in our society at the present time is what I would call the deification of science. When I talk about "science," I'm talking about the desire to know. That is perfectly legitimate. It is something that God apparently implanted in human beings. He gave us intelligence, presumably in order that we might use it. When science had its origins, it was a branch of philosophy. There was moral philosophy, metaphysical philosophy, and natural philosophy. Natural philosophy eventually began to be known as science.

But science, in its origins, was tied to a tremendous desire to understand the mysteries of being and the mysteries of existence. Originally it was philosophical, and it was deeply rooted in solid theological thinking. But in more modern times, this idea of a deep desire to understand the mystery of being has been superseded by a practical materialistic technology. And the idea is, how can we find out more to serve the purposes of man?

In its origins, science had a desire to understand the mysteries of existence, but somewhere along the line, the objectives changed. Now there are still people like Dr. Stephen W. Hawking who would say, "The eventual goal of science is to provide a single theory that describes the whole universe." That is pure science. And to the extent that that is the goal of science, how can a man or woman of faith have any disagreement with it at all? However, we know it isn't quite that straightforward. Many objections are being aimed at

39

what the Bible says about the meaning of existence and the unified theory of existence.

The rise of relativism

Albert Einstein was the one who discovered through brilliant deduction the theory of relativity. He insisted that it be tested empirically, suggested various experiments, and said quite categorically, "If anything shows that my theory is incorrect, we will discard the theory." There was an honest, genuine scientist at work. When it was eventually possible for them to set up the experimentation, the experiments established that the hypotheses were not disproven, and accordingly the theory of relativity gained general acceptance.

This made quite a dramatic change because, up until that time, Newtonian physics had held sway. But while Newtonian physics espoused many things that were true, the theory of relativity came alongside, a scientific theory. What happened, however, was that the scientific theory of relativity degenerated into a philosophy, or if you like, a theology of relativism. Paul Johnson, in his book *Modern Times,* says, "At the beginning of the 1920s, the belief began to circulate that there were no longer any absolutes of time and space, of good and evil, of knowledge, and above all, of values."

No absolutes. Relativity became confused with relativism. No one was more distressed than Einstein by this public misunderstanding. He believed, passionately, in absolute standards of right and wrong. But he lived to see moral relativism, to him a disease, become a social pandemic. Regarded by most as the greatest physicist of his generation and probably many more generations, Albert Einstein wished many times at the end of his life that he'd been just a simple watchmaker. Why? Because his scientific theory of relativity had developed and degenerated into a general philosophy of relativism, which he totally, strongly, repudiated.

Now the scientific theory of relativity in the movement of the planets has been moved into a denial of absolutes. Relativism is rampant in our society, and the result is, anything goes. And it had its roots in a scientific theory. Scientific theories certainly have their place in the scheme of things. But we must take exception to a theory of science that is allowed to become an all-pervasive philosophy, particularly when that all-pervasive philosophy flatly contradicts what Scripture teaches.

Scripture teaches absolute standards. Scripture teaches that there is good and there is evil, that there is right and there is wrong. Relativism banishes all these things and discards them on the dust heap. If we are going to stand firm on biblical revelation, we have to be able to cope with the abuse of scientific theory. Science has become, in many people's eyes, scientism. The theory of relativity has become, for many people, relativism. This idea has become almost universally accepted, and Einstein himself called it the social disease.

Evolutionism and origins

Darwin, after he made his boat trip out to the islands of South America, came back and wrote his famous book, *The Origin of the Species.* The Darwinian theory of evolution then became well known. Whether warmly responded to or violently opposed, it became highly controversial. Let me point out to you, however, that the theory of evolution has in many instances become a philosophy of evolutionism. And this philosophy of evolutionism at many points flatly contradicts biblical revelation. Where the philosophy of evolutionism contradicts biblical revelation many tend simply to discard the biblical revelation.

Professor Richard Bube of Stanford University, said this:

I believe that evolutionary theory is all too often presented as some kind of an absolutely infallible law, free from all possibility of future contradiction. Evolution has assumed the proportions of a religious faith. In the teaching of evolution, what we can say about the processes going on at the present is the most solidly based, what we can say about processes in the

41

immediate past is probably largely valid, what we can say about processes in the distant past becomes increasingly speculative, and we can say nothing scientific at all about absolute origins.

But then he adds these interesting words: "Yet the typical discussion of evolution starts the other way around." In other words, the typical discussion of evolution starts with origins, makes categorical statements about origins on the theory of evolution, and assumes everything automatically follows. When people buy into this and see it as a flat contradiction of biblical revelation, the net result is a discarding of what the Bible says.

Let me give you two examples of this kind of thinking. Carl Becker, who writes a history of science, said,

Edit and interpret the conclusions of modern science as tenderly as we like; it is still quite impossible for us to regard man as a child of God, for whom the earth was created as a temporary habitation. Rather, we must regard him as little more than a chance deposit on the surface of the world carelessly thrown up between two ice ages by the same forces that rust iron and ripen corn.

That's an eminent scientist making theory into powerful dogmatic statements concerning man.

But if you think that's a powerful dogmatic statement, let me give you another one from Dr. Jacques Monod, the French research scientist and Nobel prize winner.

Chance alone is at the source of all creation, pure chance, absolutely free but blind, at the very root of this stupendous edifice of evolution. This central concept of modern biology is no longer one among other possible or even conceivable hypotheses. It is the sole conceivable hypothesis. And nothing warrants the supposition or the hope that on this score our position is likely ever to be revised.

If Newton had talked like that, they'd have laughed him out of court, especially if the theory of relativity was in vogue! But here a Nobel scientist says there's absolutely no possibility of the theory of evolution ever being changed. That chance, blind chance, is the reason for everything, and there is no other hypothesis. How in the world does he know that? And yet people buy into this kind of thinking, turning the theory of evolution into a philosophy of evolutionism, just as the theory of relativity has become a philosophy of relativism. Science is god in our modern world.

Today the believer who stands up and says, "I believe in God the Father Almighty, maker of heaven and earth" had better recognize that a lot of people are going to regard that statement with the utmost skepticism, if not total derision. And as a result of that, they're going to have to go back to their drawing board and find out if they really do believe in a maker of all things. Why? Because our world deserves to have people who believe what they believe and know why they believe it and can articulate it.

Created in God's Image

We've focused on the maker; now let's move slightly to focus on humankind. When the Bible says, "In the beginning God created the heavens and earth," the expression "heaven and earth" means all things. And the Bible is very explicit that an intricate part of the divine creation is humankind. Genesis 1:27 says, "So God created man in his own image, in the image of God he created him; male and female he created them." Man and woman are created in the divine image.

Created by God

There are many theories about the beginning of humankind. Desmond Morris, a highly regarded zoologist, did a lot of research into man as being part of the animal kingdom. He showed how, for instance, it is perfectly apparent to everybody who thinks, that there is a clear link between humans and animals: physicians and researchers use animals to experiment on before they do anything to us because there are marked similarities in the physiology of animals and people. Desmond Morris is surely right on this point. However, he goes on to say that "we are a naked ape," which I could live with, but then he says, "and nothing more." That I can't live with. That I am an integrated part of the creation, that I am part of the animal kingdom—I have no problem accepting that at all. But if they tell me that I am an animal and nothing more, at that point I can't agree with them, because I believe that I was created uniquely, divinely, as part of the creation, but in the divine image. And this makes me separate, different, and distinct from the rest of creation.

Commissioned by God

Not only were we created in the divine image, but Genesis 1:28 tells me that we were commissioned. "God blessed them" (that is, male and female) "and said to them, 'be fruitful and increase in number; fill the earth and subdue it.' " That statement, of course, tells us that we are not just thrown up as an accident by the same forces that rust metal and ripen corn between two ice ages. It tells us that we were created by the One who is pre-existent, for a purpose, and his purpose was that we should rule and reign and administer his creation. What a noble position. That is the biblical statement concerning humans: that we are created in the divine image and commissioned to be the divine agent of all that he's created.

Commanded by God

Thirdly, humans were commanded. Genesis 2:17 tells us that God gave great freedom to man but told him that he must not eat from the tree of knowledge of good and evil. If he did, he would surely die. There's a reason for this. Man and woman were created dependent. They were created to acknowledge the sovereignty of God, that is, to be obedient. The opportunity for humans to be dependent and obedient required the opportunity for them to be independent and disobedient, and so they were given total freedom and just one test case: "Don't do that, and by refusing to do it, prove your obedience and prove your dependence." Not only that, humans were shown to be responsible, accountable, intelligent, and volitional, and to have the capacity to honor God. All this was wrapped up in this simple command.

Genesis 3:24 tells us that the people God had created chose independence over dependence, chose disobedience over obedience, rejected divine authority, paddled their own canoe, and died. Hence, the individual emptiness that is clearly catalogued in a million lives around us. Hence, the societal disintegration of order. Hence, the ecological disaster. How else do we describe what is happening in our world? People, created in the divine image, commissioned by divine fiat, commanded to live dependently and obediently, disobeyed and now live east of Eden, condemned.

Genesis 12, however, tells us of a covenant-making God who comes to disobedient, independent man and offers once again to have man reconciled to himself. God begins to call Abraham to be a member of his covenant people on the understanding that as he calls Abraham, so people from all nations of the world will respond to his call and acknowledge him as creator and redeemer. There's the story of humanity in a nutshell in Scripture. And we haven't gotten out of Genesis. That's the biblical revelation as we focus on the idea of the Maker making humans.

Making Gods of Ourselves

But what is the modern reaction? The modern reaction is probably summarized in a very ancient statement by a Greek philosopher called Protagoras, who in the fifth century B.C. said, "Man is the measure of all things." In other words, man is the standard, the criterion, the focus—essentially, he is what matters. Not God, man. This is what we call the deification of humankind. Today it has become increasingly sophisticated and increasingly the norm.

So when we stand up in our society and say, "I believe in God the Father Almighty, maker of heaven and earth," what we're really saying is, I believe in God the Father, who among other things made humankind. But we're saying that in a world that basically disagrees because it doesn't deify the maker—it deifies man. In our society, whatever the protestations about believing in God might be, when push comes to shove, man is god. This is where the challenge of being a Christian in today's world really begins to put rubber on the road.

Let me illustrate this just in one area of our society—the universities. Peter Wilkes, who once was on the staff of our church, was at one time a professor of nuclear engineering at the University of Wisconsin. In his book, *Christianity Challenges the Universe,* he wrote this,

> All cultures have their gods, and the god of secular culture is man. In the secular culture of today's university, every value becomes subordinated to that god. Culture itself is defended as worthwhile because it belongs to man. The only knowledge that matters is knowledge that directly benefits or glorifies man. The basis for morals is man, man, man.

Peter is right. The god of secular culture is man. To give you some idea of how dramatically things have changed, let me give you this quote concerning the universities in North America: "Within forty years of the landing at Plymouth Rock, the Puritans

46

turned to the task of educating what they call their learned clergy and their lettered people." The outcome was the founding of Harvard University in 1636. Harvard was one hundred years old before there was even one professor who was not a minister of religion. Harvard's original charter contains the following educational mandate: "Everyone shall consider the main end of his life and studies to know Jesus Christ, which is eternal life." This is the basic statement of Harvard University.

When Harvard professors began to lose their zeal for the faith, Yale was founded. Of the first 119 colleges founded in the United States, 104 were started by Christians to acquaint students with the knowledge of God; these included Princeton, Dartmouth, Columbia, Harvard, and Yale.

That's where the university started in America. There was a very real sense of God being God and the integrating factor of all education. University meant something then; it was the idea of unified study with a central integrating factor—the queen of sciences that was known as theology. Theology was that from which everything else came and to which everything else fitted. Uni-versity: There was a sense in which God was God. But now in the universities, man is god. This is not knocking universities; it is simply illustrating one aspect of a development in our society.

And if I'm going to say, I believe in God the Father Almighty, maker of heaven and earth including man, what I need to ask myself is this: Do I really believe in God as God of man, or when push comes to shove, do I really believe that man is god?

Not only is there the deification of man, but also a deification of man's institutions. So when we have problems, we look to institutional solutions. We look to political systems; we look to modern technology; we look to education. We still have the naive belief that whatever the problem might be, if only we educate people enough, the problem will be solved. However, there is evidence to the contrary on every hand. Deification of man and deification of man's institutions is probably one of the ultimate insults to the maker of heaven and earth.

Making Gods of Things

Finally, let's focus on matter. The biblical revelation is this: that matter is created and is not infinite. That follows from our simple reading of Genesis chapter 1. The Bible also tells us that matter is good and not evil. That comes from the statement that God made after he'd made everything; he pronounced it good. And it also teaches us in Scripture that matter is a plurality, not a unity. You'll notice that God differentiates between himself and what he's created, and he differentiates by dividing this from that and that from that, all these things to remind us that we do not accept some of the fundamental tenets of New Age thinking and New Age teaching.

What is the modern reaction, however, to this biblical revelation? One is that matter is all that matters. Or, as some people say, "The best things in life are things." That's the creed of the materialist. I will submit to you that another of the great tragedies in our society, besides the philosophies of relativism and evolutionism, is the philosophy of materialism. All of these strike at this fundamental belief in God the Father, maker of heaven and earth. If my doctrine is "Matter is all that matters" or my lifestyle simply says it, then I'm way off beat.

Let me conclude by putting the focus on you and me. What do I really believe about the maker? I love what happened in the final chapters of Job. Job was ill, having a hard time, asking all kinds of philosophical questions, and his friends "gathered around him," arguing and debating and making things ten times worse. It was like when a lot of well-meaning Christians gather around and say the most stupid things when people are hurting. And in the end, I just got the feeling that God said, "I've had it with these guys," and he leaned out of heaven, parted the clouds, rolled up his sleeves, and said, "You gentlemen down there, will you please shut up and sit down; I'm going to tell you something."

And then he embarks on the most phenomenal statement as maker of heaven and earth. He asks questions like this: "And where were you smart-alecks when I made that? How in the world did I manage without you? Seeing you're so smart and you've got all the answers, how come I did so well without your advice?" (This is paraphrased.) The net result is that Job gets the message and begins to realize that in all this debating, discussion, and independent thinking, he's been overlooking something: that behind all things, there is a great maker, to whom he owes his allegiance.

This is a great climax to the book of Job. Job answers, I've heard of you, but *now I see you.* I repent in dust and ashes.

I submit to you one of the great needs in our world today, in our society in particular, is for people to see the maker of heaven and earth and repent—repent that they put man in God's place; repent that they put matter in God's place—and make sure that the maker is the one they truly worship.

MAKING IT PRACTICAL

1. What does it mean when we say we believe God created the universe *ex nihilo?*

2. What was the original purpose of science? How has this changed?

3. What are some of the things that have been put in the place of God in our society today? How does this happen?

4. What are some ways we can reclaim God's original purpose for creating heaven, earth, and ourselves?

4

"Jesus Christ, His Only Son, Our Lord"

John 5:17-23

Believing in Jesus Christ, God's only Son, our Lord, is a big subject for a very limited amount of space. I'm reminded of the story of the cowboy who rode into town and hitched his horse up outside of the saloon, got his feed bag, and put it over his horse's head. The town drunk, who was standing nearby, said, "Any fool can see you're never going to get that horse in that bag." I feel as if I'm going to try and get a horse in a bag where it won't go, tackling this subject in only one chapter. But we will see what we can do with it.

Christ's uniqueness

It is not uncommon to find people who believe in God, but who do not believe that Jesus Christ was God's Son. In John 5:23, Jesus said, If you don't honor me, you don't really honor the Father. As soon as we look at the statements Christ made concerning himself, we realize that the distinctive of Christianity lies in the person of Jesus Christ.

J. I. Packer says, "When the creed called God maker of heaven and earth, it parted company with Hinduism and Eastern faiths in general. Now by calling Jesus Christ God's only Son, it parts company with Judaism and Islam and stands quite alone."

In our pluralistic society, where we have a great desire to be tolerant and open to everybody's point of view, sometimes the distinctives of what we believe are blurred. And when that is the case, then, of course, we can finish up in a nonsensical position. For instance, the Eastern religions would have us believe, not that God created things independently of himself and that they are separate from him; rather, they would want us to believe that all is God. But if we believe that God is the maker of heaven and earth, we immediately put some distance between ourselves and Eastern belief. The great religions of Islam and Judaism do not accept that Jesus is the Son of God. So if we believe that Jesus is the only begotten Son of God, then automatically we do not accept what Islam and Judaism preach. So however much we want to agree with everybody and sort of synchronize all these religions, if we are convinced in our hearts concerning the fundamentals of the Christian faith, we find Christianity utterly distinct. And we take our stand upon it.

Christ is controversial

To say that Jesus Christ is controversial is to make the greatest of all understatements. Let me give you two examples of the controversial nature of Jesus. Years ago at Oxford University, there was a young student called Algernon Swinburne. He was well known for his brilliant poetry, and it was popular among the students; not infrequently they would gather together and learn some of his poems by heart. Because they were rhythmic, students would march up and down the streets of Oxford chanting his poetry.

One of his most famous statements is this:

"Thou has conquered, pale Galilean;
the world has grown grey from thy breath."

Swinburne was not just an atheist; he was anti-theist. You can have an atheist who says he believes there is no God, but you can have an anti-theist who is vehemently opposed to any concept of God. Swinburne was particularly opposed to any concept of Christ being the Son of God and Christianity being true. In fact, he makes a damning statement concerning his perception of Christ and his church. He calls Christ the "pale Galilean," and says that wherever he's gone, things have "grown grey" with his breath. I know people today who take vehement opposition to the person of Jesus Christ because they totally dislike all that he says, all that he stands for, and all that he taught. They cannot bear the thought that he is our Savior.

In marked contrast to that, Dorothy L. Sayers said this concerning Christ and the church: "We have very efficiently pared the claws of the lion of Judah, certified him meek and mild, and recommended him as a fitting household pet for pale curates and pious old ladies." That's similar to the pale Galilean idea. However, she goes on to say, "To those who knew him, however, Jesus Christ in no way suggested a milk and water person. They objected to him as a dangerous firebrand. He was emphatically not a dull man in his human lifetime."

Was Jesus a pale Galilean who has made the world gray through his breath? Or was he a firebrand who has set the world aflame? These are the kind of polarized positions that you find concerning Jesus Christ. When we profess, "I believe in Jesus Christ, his only Son, our Lord," we need to ask ourselves, *What do I believe about Jesus Christ, his only Son, our Lord?*

The name *Christ* means "Messiah." And so, when we talk of Jesus Christ, we first of all think in terms of the Messiahship of Christ. When we talk about his only Son, we focus on the sonship of Christ. And, of course, when we talk about him being Lord, we focus on the lordship of Christ. These are the three areas that I want to discuss with you in this chapter.

Jesus As Messiah

Jesus was a very common name at the time Jesus Christ was born. And in parts of Latin America today, it is still a common name. If you watch boxing, you'll find many Latin American boxers are called Jesus. It always seems strange to me to see somebody called Jesus beating up on somebody called Jesus. But it is just a common name. The name Jesus, however, is full of significance.

There's a song we sometimes sing in Christian congregations that begins, "Jesus, Jesus, Jesus, there's just something about that name." It's one of those quiet, meditative songs that sort of helps the congregation mellow out. But I don't get very mellow when we're singing it because I get frustrated. I'm waiting for somebody to tell me what this something is about that name, but the song never does. It leaves me hanging: there's just something about that name. I want something specific about that name!

Jesus As Savior

The name *Jesus* is Greek for the Hebrew name *Joshua*. And *Joshua* means "God is Savior." The unique thing about the baby born of Mary in Bethlehem nineteen hundred years ago is that his name really describes who he is: "God is Savior." Notice the emphasis on God. It points out the eternal significance of this name. There *is* something about his name. When we say "Jesus," we say God, the eternal one, is eternally committed to the salvation of human beings. In Matthew chapter 1, when the baby was named, it was said he would be called Jesus, for he would save his people from their sins. Notice the universal significance of this name. It reminds us that God, the eternal one, is concerned to save his people out of every kindred and tongue and tribe and nation.

Out of every generation there will be people who will be impacted by the person of Jesus the Savior. Notice the social significance. He comes to save his people from their sins. The root meaning of the word *save* in Hebrew is "room or space or width." The idea of salvation is that it frees people up; it gives them space, room, opportunity for growth. Unfortunately, people either have been given or have gained the impression that salvation is a crimping and a cramping thing. The converse is the truth. Jesus, the

Savior, God manifest in the flesh, comes into society in order that he might free people and give them space to breathe and room to grow, the opportunity to develop fully as the people they're intended to be.

Salvation does not give me the kind of width and space that gives me "freedom to be me." Instead it gives me freedom and space to be all that God created me to be in the first place. And therein lies fullness of life. What a tragedy that Christianity is seen by some and portrayed by many as being a cramping and a limiting faith.

Charles Wesley got the picture right when he said in his hymn, "And Can It Be That I Should Gain?":

Long my imprisoned spirit lay
Fast bound in sin and nature's night.
Thine eye diffused a quickening ray;
I woke—the dungeon flamed with light!
My chains fell off, my heart was free,
I rose, went forth, and followed Thee.

That is what *Jesus* means: God saving people from their sins.

There are many ways in which salvation is being applied today. In some areas of the world, people talk about liberation theology. They see salvation as a means of liberating people from political and economic oppression. Granted, Christ is concerned about justice and stands against injustice, but simply to suggest that salvation means freedom from political and economic woes is to miss the point. Christ's salvation deals with sin, that which brings guilt and shame and oppression and injustice. It is not oppression and injustice that are the problem. It is human sin that perpetrates the injustice and the oppression. And he came to deal with the root condition of people. This is what is in the name Jesus. Jesus is Savior.

So next time you sing "Jesus, Jesus, Jesus, there's just something about that name," you know what some of the something is. When we say we believe, however, in Jesus Christ, we're going a step further. For if Jesus is his name, Christ is his title. And these are two things that we need to be clear about.

Let me give you an example. I was talking to a friend of mine, and he told me how he had been personally invited to Washington to be presented to President Reagan. He spoke with great delight and pride about that moment. One could understand why. And then he said this: "I was never a great fan of Reagan as a person or as a policy maker, so I wasn't particularly interested in meeting Ronald Reagan, but I was so excited to meet the president." *President Reagan* spoke of office as well as person. *Jesus Christ* also speaks of person and of office.

Christ, the anointed one

What do we mean by *Christ?* The Greek word from which we get our English word *Christ* is *Christos.* And that is the equivalent of the Anglicized Hebrew word *Messiah*—literally meaning "the anointed one." The idea is of somebody who is God's special ambassador with a particular ministry in mind. That the Messiah was expected in the days of Jesus and had been long expected in previous generations is abundantly clear from Scripture.

On one occasion the Lord Jesus stopped off in Samaria, which in itself was a surprise because Jews didn't go through Samaria. He went to a well mid-day and got into a conversation with a woman, which was another surprise because men didn't approach women in those days. This woman had a very disreputable character, and that was yet another surprise. But during the course of this surprising interview where Jesus carefully tramples over all kinds of traditions, the lady says to Jesus at one point, "I know that when the Messiah, that is Christ, comes, he will show us all things." Now here's a Samaritan, who has no love for the Jews, saying that the Jewish Messiah is coming. We expect him to come, and we also know that when he comes, he will show us all things. She meant "there are many things that we do not understand about God, but he is going to send his specially anointed one, and when he comes, we will have a par-excellence revelation of the person of God himself." So there was a keen expectation that Messiah, or Christ, would come.

When I say I believe in Jesus Christ, what I'm saying is I believe that the baby of Bethlehem, "God is Savior," came from the Father expressly in order that he might reveal the hidden father—par excellence. This expected Christ was deeply respected too. There was a certain majesty about this title, about his office. When Peter preached on the day of Pentecost, he culminated his address with these words, "Therefore, let all the house of Israel know assuredly that God has made this Jesus, whom you crucified, both Lord and Christ." What a striking thing to say: to tell them that they had crucified Jesus, and of course, they had, just a few weeks earlier, within a few yards of where he was speaking! But to say that the one they had crucified was in actual fact the Christ, the Messiah, was deeply disturbing to them. We read in Acts chapter 2 their reaction—when they heard this they were deeply cut in their hearts. Why? Because there was a deep respect for the expected Messiah. So when we say Jesus Christ is the one in whom we believe, we're talking about the long-expected, deeply respected one who had come from the Father in order to reveal him par excellence.

Christ, the prophet

The word *Christ* not only speaks of his office, but gives us a clue to what his office involved. "The anointed one" is the key. There were three kinds of people in the Old Testament who were anointed as an evidence of their office: prophets, priests, and kings. Put in very simple terms, the prophet was somebody who would bring God to man. God, when he wanted to speak to people, would often raise up a prophet, give the prophet a message, and say, "Go to the people." Often it was a very unpopular message, and so the life expectancy of a prophet was short indeed. And life insurance was extremely expensive. However, these courageous people would go to the people, and they would preface their remarks with "Thus saith the Lord." In other words, they were bringing the word of God to man.

There has always been a desire on the part of men and women to have a word from outside, an authoritative, comforting, directing word. In the old days it used to be the prophets. Now we have horoscopes. And I'm utterly incredulous that people actually believe them, which indicates how desperate people are, deep in their souls, for directional, comforting, and encouraging words.

Not only do people go to their horoscopes nowadays; they go to mediums. Well, they used to go to mediums; now they go to "channelers." Basically they're the same thing. It's just that the word *channeler* fits better in our television age. New Age people are very much into channeling.

The idea of a channeler is that in some way or other, he or she gets in touch with what is described as an "entity." This "entity" speaks through the medium, or channeler, and brings a prophetic, an authoritative, a directive, or a comforting word. And there are many, many people who are looking for this kind of a word.

A friend of Shirley MacLaine explains it as follows: "Entities, or spirit beings, have important implications to us as human beings because of the insight and factual information that comes through them." These entities claim to be all kinds of people; some even claim to be Christ himself.

One channeler, speaking allegedly on behalf of Christ, has been uttering things that are in dramatic opposition to all that Christ ever said. For instance, Christ, through one of the channelers, is reputedly saying, "The sayings in the Epistles and in the Gospels and the Revelation to the effect that my blood saves from sin are totally erroneous."

People are looking for a prophetic word. They're looking at horoscopes, they're going to mediums, they are getting into channeling. They want a word from out there.

But let me remind you that if you believe in Jesus Christ, the anointed one, the prophet, there's word enough in him. Tear up your horoscope, point out the fallacy to your channeling friends, and stand firm, believing in Jesus Christ, God's prophet, the priest.

Christ, the priest and king

The priest brings man to God. He is the mediator, the intermediary. He is the one who takes man where he is, takes him by the hand, and leads him into the presence of God. So if a prophet brings God to man, a priest brings man to God. And this was the office of Jesus, the Christ. He was the one who took away the barrier of sin and brought people into an experience where they could know the living and true God.

The anointed one was also a king. In the Old Testament a king was often seen as a shepherd of the people as well. He would lead, guide, and direct people into the ways of God. So Christ comes, claiming to be the anointed one, and in so doing says, "I am the long expected, deeply respected one whose office is to bring God to man, bring man to God, and lead men and women, boys and girls, into the path of righteousness for his name's sake." So when I say I believe in Jesus Christ, that's what is meant by it from a biblical standpoint. Can *you* say, "I believe in Jesus Christ and his Messiahship?"

Jesus As God's Son

I believe in Jesus Christ, *his only son*. The little word *only* seems superfluous there, like it's just there for padding. But I assure you it isn't. On more than one occasion in Scripture, Jesus is described as "the only begotten." To be begotten means to be born. The other old-fashioned word that you find in the genealogies of the Bible is *begat*. "So and so begat so and so, and so and so begat so and so." There was an awful lot of begetting going on in those days. And everybody who begot was begotten. The idea was that they were born of their father.

When the Bible says that Jesus is the only begotten of the Father, this has led people to say, "Well, if Jesus was begotten of the Father, he must have had a mother. And who was his mother?" Some people have, therefore, put two and two together and come up with the wonderful answer that God the father had a wife called the virgin mother, and they had an infant Jesus, and together the three make up the holy trinity.

That is the fallacy that has led Islam to flatly reject Jesus as the Son of God, because they see his only begottenship as being a purely physical thing—God having sex with a virgin and producing the infant Jesus. They say, "That is repugnant, that is totally unacceptable, and we reject it."

If you talk to a Jehovah's Witness, or more accurately, if you listen to a Jehovah's Witness, you discover that they love to take you to these "begotten" passages. They say, "There you are; he can't be God because he is begotten of God, he is born, he is created like anything else."

Understanding Christ's begottenness is a crucial foundation of Christianity, so we must address it. The Greek word translated as "the only begotten" is *monogēnas*. If you forget all of the rest of the Greek you know, remember *monogēnas*. Mono as in *monologue*—one person doing all the talking, as opposed to dialogue, where we have a conversation. *Mono,* therefore, means "one." *Gēnas* is the word from which we get *genes* or *genetic* or *gender*. It has to do with kind or nature. I am what I am to a certain extent because of my genetic structure. Where did I get my genetic structure from? I got my genetic structure from my parents. I am of a kind with them. I am of the same nature as them—and like them.

"You do look like your father," people tell me when I go back to England. Others say, "No, he looks like his mother." But in actual fact, I probably don't look like my mother as far as the beard is concerned, but my eyes and cheekbones perhaps do. I am of a kind, of a nature, of an essence, of my parents. That's what *gēnas* means.

Monogēnas means, literally, "one of a kind." When it says that Jesus is the only begotten Son, it is not talking about him being created, as being inferior to God. It's saying exactly the opposite. He is of the same kind, the same genes, the same nature, the same essence of God. He is God. But there's only one of him; he is unique. He is uniquely God demonstrated in human form.

That's very important because it's at this point that Christianity must take a stand. For there are many, many other people who will believe in a vague creator and maker, who believe as the Muslims do, that Jesus was virgin born, was a prophet, and that he is the Messiah, but who don't believe that he is God himself manifest in the flesh.

The wonder of this comes through in John 3:16: "God so loved the world that he gave his *monogēnas* Son." What does it mean that he *gave* him? It means that he gave him up to death on the cross. And the foundation of the Christian faith is that Jesus Christ, the only begotten of the Father, one of a kind, God himself, died on the cross on our behalf. Some people have objected to the doctrine of the Atonement, saying that God was all holy and man was all sinful, so God looked around for some poor unsuspecting character that he could kill on the cross for people's sins. That absolutely is not true, for when Christ dies on the cross, he is one of a kind with the Father. It is God himself who bears our sins in his own body on the tree.

Now we can sing "Jesus, Jesus, Jesus, there's just something about his name." Next time we sing it, our minds are going to be absolutely buzzing with something. For he is God who is Savior, who is Christ, who is only begotten Son.

Jesus As Lord

Finally, we come to the third point concerning Jesus, and that is his lordship. I believe in Jesus Christ, his only Son, *our Lord*. Now, the Greek word for Lord is *kurios*. When the Old Testament was translated into Greek, it was reportedly translated by seventy translators; hence it is called the Septuagint. It's very interesting to notice the Greek words that we use to translate the Hebrew words. The Hebrew word *Adonai,* which was translated "Lord" in the Old Testament in reference to God, was translated in the Greek New Testament *kurios.* So when you read *Lord* applied to Jesus in the New Testament, there's a clear link with the Old Testament statement concerning deity. That Jesus is deity is clearly seen in the use of *kurios* as applied to him. And some people will say, "Jesus never claimed to be God overtly." That may or may not be the case, but there's abundant evidence that he was convinced that he was Lord, *kurios.*

For instance, on one occasion he said to his disciples, "You call me master and Lord and rightly so." On another occasion when Thomas doubted whether Jesus was risen from the dead, he stipulated what it would take for him to believe. Then when Jesus showed up, Thomas fell at his feet and said, "My Lord and my God!"

And Jesus said, "Don't say that. Good night! You're going to get us all into trouble. I don't want anybody saying I'm Lord. And I certainly don't want anybody saying I'm God. Do you realize what's going to happen if these Jewish religious leaders hear you saying that? You dummy. Don't you say that again."

No. He didn't say that. He stood there and allowed Thomas to kneel at his feet and say, "My Lord and my God!" He affirmed him. Jesus Christ simply and clearly claimed to be Lord.

Some people believe in Jesus Christ as a figure of history. And some historians point out to us that in actual fact there's more historical evidence concerning Jesus Christ as a person who actually lived than there is concerning Julius Caesar. So you don't need to be very smart to say, "I believe in Jesus Christ as a historical personage." But if we simply leave it at that and say, "Well, he walked around two thousand years ago in the Middle East, and he was a great moral teacher," then our thinking is incomplete. That's where a lot of people get stuck.

We, as Christians, need to be able to communicate to people who are in that place. C. S. Lewis says it best:

Any man who is merely a man and said the sort of things Jesus said would not be a great moral teacher. He would either be a lunatic on a level with the man who says he is a poached egg, or else he would be the devil of hell. You must make your choice. You can shut him up for a fool, you can spit on him and kill him as a demon, or you can fall at his feet and call him Lord and God. But let us not come with any patronizing nonsense about his being a great human teacher. He has not left that open to us, he did not intend to.

In other words, Jesus Christ backs you firmly into a corner. He stands there and he says, "Look at me; I and the Father are one. If you've seen me, you've seen the Father. The Father has committed all judgment into my hands. No one has seen the Father except the Son, who's come from the Father. I am the way, the truth and the life. No one comes to the Father but by me." That is Jesus Christ's teaching.

What do you make of this great moral teaching? If it's true, it's more than great moral teaching; it is God introducing himself to us in human form. So we don't call him a great moral teacher; we bow before him and say, "Our Lord and God!" But what if it's untrue? What if he isn't all that he says he is? Then he is on the level of the man who says, "I am a poached egg." In other words, he's crazy, or he is a total reprobate renegade, the greatest con-artist of all time.

Jesus Christ backs us into a corner and says, "Will you please make up your mind and be done with this patronizing nonsense of suggesting I'm a great moral teacher, and would you decide, please, if I'm crazy, or if I'm a crook, or if I'm Christ." That's where he puts us. Therefore, when we think in terms of Jesus claiming to be Lord, we have to come to an intelligent conclusion. But more than that; we have to make a moral conclusion as well. For we're required to confess Christ as Lord and to treat him as Lord.

A practical application of this word *Lord* is seen in Luke's gospel, when Jesus was getting ready for Palm Sunday. He needed transport to get into Jerusalem so he said to two of his disciples, "Go to the house over there, and outside you'll find a little donkey; untie it and bring it to me." They were doing that, and Luke tells us that when the owners saw them taking away the donkey, they said, "What are you doing?" And they replied, "The Lord has need of him." The Greek word translated "owners" is *kurioi*. The Greek word translated "Lord" is *kurios*. The one is the plural of the other. *Lord,* in this context, means "owner."

The practical application of Christ's lordship is his ownership of our lives. We come to an intelligent conclusion concerning his lordship because we've decided that he isn't a crook and he isn't crazy; he's Christ the Lord. But we go a step further and say, If it is true that he is Lord, then he must take ownership of my life. I give him my allegiance. I believe, not only in God the Father Almighty, maker of heaven and earth, but also in Jesus Christ his only Son, our Lord.

When Jill and I got married, I was a young banker and Jill was a young schoolteacher. We needed a house in Manchester, where I'd been transferred by the bank, and because they brought me in from another town, they helped me a little bit. And this is how they did it. The bank would sometimes have to repossess houses where the mortgage had been in default. Banks, in those days, hated to repossess. It was terribly embarrassing to them. But if the house was the only collateral they had, they sometimes did it most reluctantly. Then they didn't know what to do with the houses. So they would take them and make them available to young people like me who they'd transferred in from another town. They gave this house to us at the principal rent of twelve shillings and sixpence a week, which in those days was approximately two dollars a week, about what it was worth, and about what we could afford.

There was only one problem, however. Here we were, a young married couple, embarking on living happily ever after, but the previous tenant wouldn't get out. Although the house was ours, we couldn't take possession of it. So I talked to Jill about it, and I said,

"It is very awkward, Jill, because the previous tenant won't get out."

"Well," she said, "tell him to get out."

I said, "It's a little awkward. He's my boss."

And she said, "What's he doing in there anyway? He doesn't need to be in cheap housing like that."

I said, "He's cheap. He's my boss and he's cheap. And I can't get him out."

She said, "What are we going to do?"

I said, "Well, I could talk to him and see if we could move in with him."

She said, "Absolutely not." She didn't seem to think that was a very good idea, which is true of a number of my ideas. I remember her saying, "It's just not fair."

And I said, "Jill, you're absolutely right. There's no justice in this thing at all. That's our house. And this person won't get out. He is keeping possession of what isn't his."

It is not fair that some people say, "I believe in Jesus Christ, God's only Son, my Lord," and they keep possession of what they say is his. To profess Jesus Christ as Lord means I've arrived at an intelligent conclusion that he was not crazy and he was not a crook. Therefore, he was who he claimed to be. And I take it to its logical conclusion. And I say, "My Lord and my God." That's what it means to believe in Jesus Christ, his only Son, our Lord.

MAKING IT PRACTICAL

1. What makes Christianity different from other religions?

2. What does the name *Jesus* mean? What does *Christ* mean? What is the significance of these two parts of his name?

3. What are some of the reasons people have for rejecting the idea that Jesus was "begotten of the Father"? What does the Greek word for "the only begotten," *monogēnas,* really mean?

4. If we believe that Jesus is Lord, we believe he has ownership of our lives. In what ways can we show that we consider him the owner of our lives?

5

"Born of the
Virgin Mary"

Matthew 1:18-25

Sometimes people are very tolerant of what we believe; sometimes they're quite opposed to what we believe. We need to know how to respond if we are to communicate effectively the Christian faith, which, of course, is one of our high and noble privileges. We need to know what we are talking about. And we need to know what people are thinking as we try to communicate with them.

When we come to this topic of the virgin birth, or, more accurately, the virgin conception of Jesus Christ, immediately we find that we are moving into areas of broad disagreement. Dr. Millard Erickson of Bethel Theological Seminary says this, "Next to the crucifixion and resurrection of Christ, perhaps the one event of his life that has received the greatest amount of attention is the virgin birth. Certainly next to the resurrection it is the most debated and controversial."

In order that we might look at this subject in a helpful manner, I want to talk first of all about the basis of the belief. Why does the Apostles' Creed state this incredible thing—that Jesus Christ was conceived of the Holy Spirit and born of the virgin Mary? What basis is there for believing this? Then we'll look at the causes of the controversy. Why is it that so much controversy swirls around this particular belief? We'll conclude by talking about the implications of the Incarnation, dealing with the biblical statement of the virgin conception of Christ and the practical implications for our lives.

The Biblical Basis for the Virgin Birth

First let's look at the basis of the belief. In Genesis chapter 3, you come across what the theologians call the *protoevangelion,* or the first hint of the *evangel,* or the gospel of Jesus Christ. It is very interesting to notice that this statement is addressed to the devil, of all people. And so in the strictest sense of the word, the first evangelistic statement was given to Satan.

The seed of the woman

You remember the background of the story. God created the universe; he created man male and female; he ordained that they should be stewards of his creation. They were clearly told that they should operate on the principle of obedience and dependence. They were tempted, and as a result of the temptation, God's sovereignty was challenged and their lives were rejected. And God immediately addressed the serpent, who was behind all this, and this is what he said:

> Because you have done this, cursed are you above all the livestock and all the wild animals! You will crawl on your belly and you will eat dust all the days of your life. And I will put enmity between you and the woman, and between your offspring and hers; he will crush your head, and you will strike his heel. *Genesis 3:14-15*

Why do we believe in the virgin birth or the virgin conception? The first answer is, "Because of this *protoevangelion,* this initial hint of what God was going to do to counter the challenge to his sovereignty." Well, what was he going to do? He was going to bring what he calls "the seed of the woman." And the seed of the woman would challenge the evil one and crush the serpent's head under his heel. However, in so doing, this seed himself would be bitten on the heel. Very dramatic, picturesque language. It's referring to Christ overcoming the evil one, crushing his power and restoring divine sovereignty, but suffering terribly himself in the course of it.

Notice the unusual description given to this one who will bruise the serpent's head. He is described as "the seed of the woman." That is most unusual. When we talk of matters of birth, if we talk about seed at all, it is always the male seed and the female receptivity of the male seed. And so those who take the Scriptures seriously would not want to build a doctrine of the virgin birth on Genesis 3:15, but they would see it as one of the basic building blocks in this belief. It is the first clue that the one God would send to overthrow Satan's rule, who would be terribly hurt in overthrowing that rule, would be of the seed of the woman. This is a clear hint to the virgin birth.

The prophecy regarding a virgin

In the book of Isaiah is a well-known prophetic statement (well known because it is lifted out of its Old Testament context and quoted by Matthew in the first chapter of his book), giving the story of the birth of Jesus. Let me remind you of the story. The people of Judah centered in the capital city of Jerusalem are under attack; their backs are to the wall, and they're in dire danger. King Ahaz doesn't know what to do. He has the prophet Isaiah alongside him.

The Lord speaks to Isaiah and says, "Go to King Ahaz and say, 'Be careful, keep calm, and don't be afraid.'" (Perhaps in modern translation, "Don't worry; be happy.")

Ahaz immediately says something to the effect of, "You've got to be kidding! Look what's going on here; terrible things are going to happen; I'm going to be ruined."

And God, through Isaiah, says, "It is not going to take place. Ask for a sign, and I'll prove it to you."

Ahaz says, "I don't want to ask for a sign."

God says, "Ask for a sign in the highest height or the deepest depth."

But Ahaz says, "I don't want to bother God, I don't want to put him to the test."

And Isaiah responds, "Are you even going to start irritating God now? Why don't you do what he tells you to do? Anyway, even if you won't ask for a sign, God's going to give you one. 'The virgin will be with child and will give birth to a son, and will call his name Immanuel.'" Notice the context in which this sign is given. It is in the context of King Ahaz being surrounded by his enemies and feeling that all is lost. Yet he is being told by God, "Don't worry; be happy; you're going to be in good shape. And I'll prove it to you: Here's the sign."

Matthew takes this particular story totally out of its context and applies it to the virgin birth and sees it as a prophetic utterance, as a prediction of what is going to happen. Those who believe that the Bible is inspired by the Holy Spirit, that Matthew is inspired and Isaiah is inspired, have no difficulty at all saying that if the Holy Spirit wants to inspire Matthew to see that meaning there, and the inspired Spirit brings it to Matthew, that's a good enough interpretation.

We have to recognize, however, that not everybody is going to be so amenable to Scripture. And those that we're trying to talk to, those who we're trying to impress with the validity of the Christian faith, are going to be somewhat skeptical. They may point out to us, for instance, that the Hebrew word translated "virgin" in Isaiah chapter 7, is the Hebrew word *alma*. And the word *alma* does not necessarily mean a virgin. It can simply mean a young woman. That is why in some versions of the Bible you will simply read that "a young woman will bear a child and will give birth to a son, and his name will be Immanuel." *Immanuel* means "God with us." So they may say to us, as many people would say, the sign was simply this, that a young woman was going to have a baby and she would call his name Immanuel, and that would be a wonderful encouragement and reminder to the people that God is with us. So you may find yourself with people who do not accept what the Scriptures are saying here at face value. But they have a point, because it is perfectly true that *alma* does not necessarily mean "virgin."

Understanding Old Testament prophecy

When we look into this whole business of Old Testament prophecy, we realize that we're in a somewhat tricky area. Let me touch on three ways of looking at this sort of statement. Some theologians talk about what they call the *sensus plenior* or the fuller sense, of Scripture. What they would say is: It may be perfectly right to say that there was an immediate fulfillment of this prediction by Isaiah; otherwise, what help would it have been to Ahaz? But, while there was an immediate fulfillment of a child being born who was called Immanuel, there is a fuller sense, there is a *sensus plenior* in this thing. While a sign came to King Ahaz immediately, the greatest sign to the house of David was that the triumph would come through Immanuel, born of the virgin, and that is a prediction of Jesus Christ. So the *sensus plenior* approach is that there can be two meanings to a prophetic statement; an immediate one and an ultimate one.

Another approach to prophecy is the *present persuader* approach. In other words, the prophet is simply talking to his contemporaries and is predicting something to persuade them to a certain course of action. So people would look at this particular statement, and they would say, Listen, what Isaiah was really saying is, "There is a virgin, who is a virgin right now, who subsequently will marry and have a child, and the child will be called Immanuel. The time needed for that will be the time that God will prove his faithfulness, and during that time you are going to be all right. And don't worry; be happy." This is the *present persuader* approach.

Then there is the *future confirmation* approach. They would interpret it this way: It really didn't have anything to do with a baby who would be born in Ahaz's time; the prophecy is all very much in

71

the future. It is a prediction concerning Jesus being born of the virgin. And the whole point of it is that God would be able to lean out of heaven and say, "I told you so! When will you guys start believing me? Hundreds of years ago I told you that this was what I was going to do, and now I've done it. Why don't you get your act together?"

So you see, when we look at prophecy in different ways, it's relatively easy to see why it is that people arrive at different conclusions concerning the Bible. If we're going to take our stand on what the Scriptures say and make protestations of faith such as, "I believe that Jesus Christ was conceived of the Holy Spirit, born of the virgin Mary," we'd better be geared up to know what the other points of view are. However, I believe firmly that the Scriptures are inspired by God and that Matthew is inspired to take this statement out of context. He sees it under the inspiration of the Holy Spirit as a specific prediction concerning the birth of Jesus. And of course, we remind ourselves of that every Christmas. So there's the second building block. The *protoevangelion* in Genesis 3:15, and then the prophecy in Isaiah chapter 7.

The pronouncements to Mary and Joseph

Next we come to the pronouncements, the first one given to Mary in Luke, and the other one given to Joseph in Matthew. In Luke's gospel there is an announcement to Mary, who is described as a virgin. The Greek word here is *parthenos*. Now people say that *parthenos* is always translated "virgin." But, in fact, it is not always translated "virgin." In the Septuagint, the Greek version of the Old Testament, there's a passage in Genesis 34:4 where Dinah, who was raped terribly, is described as a *parthenos*. Clearly, if she'd been raped, she couldn't be, in the strictest sense of the word, a virgin. So it is not true to say that *parthenos* always means "virgin." However, the weight of evidence shows that that is what is intended, because Mary uses the word herself. When she's told she's going to have a son, she says in effect, "How in the world can that happen, seeing that I am a *parthenos?*" By that she meant that she had never had sexual relations.

The announcement that is made to Joseph gets a similar response. Joseph was betrothed to Mary, and when he heard that she was with child, he wanted to divorce her. They were not married, but they were betrothed. In the marriage system of the first century, betrothal was a whole lot more serious than engagement is in our society. Betrothal meant that they were absolutely committed to each other, but for a period of time, while the preparations were going on, they would not come together in sexual union. That was betrothal. But the commitment was as solid as marriage would be with that one fundamental exception.

When Joseph hears that she is pregnant, he knows that it has nothing to do with him; therefore, the pregnancy is either what she says it is, or it is illegitimate. And if the pregnancy is illegitimate, then her activity is punishable by death. And so he decides, because he is a righteous man and goes by the law, to divorce her. Then the angel comes and says, "Don't be afraid. (Don't worry; be happy!) Everything's okay here. That which is conceived in her is conceived of the Holy Spirit."

So now we see the *protoevangelion* from Genesis, the building block of Isaiah's prediction, and then the two pronouncements that clearly make a statement concerning the virgin birth or conception of the Lord Jesus.

It has been pointed out, however, that only two of the Gospels mention the virgin birth. And people say, "That's rather strange, isn't it?" It's also been pointed out that the virgin birth is never mentioned in the evangelistic apostolic teaching, and that, for some strange reason, the virgin birth never appears in the development of the apostolic teaching. It's only mentioned twice in all four Gospels; it is never mentioned in Acts; and it doesn't rate in the Epistles either. So some people ask, "Why should this be?" Various answers come forward, and we recognize that this is a problem for some people. However, the basis for our belief is supported by the fact that, while the virgin birth is not a widespread statement in

73

Scripture, it is clearly there, and if we accept that the Scriptures are inspired by God, then we have grounds for believing it.

Causes of the Controversy

If you start talking about believing that Christ was born of the virgin Mary, you'll find a large segment of our society will say to you, "You've got to be kidding—virgins don't have babies. You should know that. I thought you were a reasonably intelligent person. How in the world did you get suckered into believing that nonsense?"

What vantage point are these people coming from? Why are they addressing it in this way? Well, they're addressing it from what we would call a naturalistic point of view. A naturalist is somebody who believes that the world, or nature, as they often call it, is a closed system, and that inside this closed system there are clearly discernible laws. One of the clearly discernible laws in this closed system of our universe is this: If you want to make a baby, you need a female ovum and a male sperm. It can't be done any other way. Therefore, for the Bible to suggest that Jesus was born of a female ovum and no male sperm is utterly, totally impossible and thoroughly ridiculous. That is the naturalist point of view.

Another approach, however, is what we call the supernaturalist point of view. The supernaturalist believes that the universe, which has clearly delineated laws of operation, was created by somebody independent of the creation. *Supernatural*—beyond the natural, above the natural. And this supernatural One who created is perfectly free to move into nature, not to change the laws, but to add things that he chooses.

C. S. Lewis helps us understand this concept when he talks about playing billiards. For the benefit of those of you who have not played billiards for a long time, let me remind you that you have a nice green table, a cue, three balls, a red one and two white ones. The idea is to hit the white cue ball with your cue and to make it collide with the red ball. A clearly discernible law of nature (or law of physics, if you like), will tell you that when the white ball collides with the red ball, the red ball will accelerate and the white ball will decelerate, and the red ball will accelerate at the same rate that the white ball will decelerate. The energy is simply transferred from the one to the other. That is a law. And naturalists will tell you, That is the only way it will work. They will go even further and say, It is impossible for a red billiard, when hit by a white billiard ball, to travel faster than the white ball is slowing down.

Lewis says, Not so. Because after I've hit my shot, I may realize I didn't hit it hard enough, so while you're turning the other way, I simply hit the red ball with my cue and I cheat. Then the red ball will go faster than the white ball is slowing down. And in his inimitable style Lewis says, "God cheats." God simply moves into the laws of nature that he has ordained and adds another factor.

So what is a miracle? A miracle is a supernatural intervention in the natural law. If I am a naturalist, then C. S. Lewis says this: If naturalism is true, then we do know in advance that miracles are impossible. Nothing can come into nature from the outside because there's nothing outside to come in. Now that is obvious. If I am a supernaturalist, though, then miracles are not impossible at all. They are highly improbable, but they are certainly possible.

Let's say that I get into a big debate with a naturalist over the impossibility of the virgin birth. And he says, "There's nothing outside the laws of nature; nothing can intervene; therefore, a miracle is impossible. Therefore, the virgin birth is impossible." But if I am a supernaturalist, I'll say, "Who made the laws? Who organized nature? Who put the whole thing together? Who keeps it going? Doesn't he have the prerogative to intervene and add another factor if he so chooses? Therefore, I see no problem at all with the possibility, albeit the total improbability of the virgin birth." And the possibility is clearly there. That's where the controversy rages with the naturalist. I guarantee that if you go out into our society today, you will find latent or actual naturalists wherever you go, who will talk loosely about miracles, but who don't really believe in supernatural intervention in the natural course of events.

Then there's another area of controversy. At the turn of the century, the churches in America were alarmed that many of their pastors were either studying in Germany or being influenced by liberal German theologians. These liberal German theologians, (their term for themselves) were doing all sorts of funny things with Scripture. They were bringing in all kinds of "critical studies" to bear upon it, and many of the people in the church in America felt that they were getting away from the authority of Scripture, and they were right. When the people decided to put a stop to this trend, a series of books called *The Fundamentals* were written, challenging the liberal trends in theology.

One of the trends in liberal theology was this: The liberal theologians would use the biblical terminology but mean entirely different things by it. So when one liberal theologian was challenged as to whether he believed in the deity of Christ, he said, "Of course I believe in the deity of Christ. I believe in the deity of every man." What he meant by the deity of Christ was miles away from the traditional belief in the deity of Christ. If he was being challenged, "Do you believe in the miraculous birth of Jesus?" He'd have said, "Of course I believe in the miraculous birth of Jesus; every birth is a miracle." He would use the same terms but mean entirely different things by them. It became a game of semantics, a game that many still play. For instance, politicians promise no new taxes. Revenue enhancement, yes! But no new taxes.

I was in South Africa when the minister of housing decided to move earth-moving equipment into a shanty town and destroy the whole thing. Some ministers I was working with decided to challenge him because he had promised he would never, ever bulldoze the shanty town. So they linked arms in front of the earth-moving equipment. The television cameras were focused, and they read the statement by this minister. He came walking by, and they challenged him. And he said, in front of the television cameras, "You should stick to preaching, because the promise was 'I will not bulldoze shanty town,' but you don't know the difference between a bulldozer and a front-end loader." He had simply put in front-end loaders to bulldoze the shanty town because he knew he'd promised not to bulldoze it.

The fundamentalists said, We have got to nail these liberal theologians to the wall, and that's like nailing jello to the wall. So they got a test case: the virgin birth of Christ. This became the test of orthodoxy. As a result, it became necessary in the early days of the century to be able to say that you categorically believed in the miraculous birth of Jesus in a unique way, and if you did you were orthodox, and if you didn't you were liberal. Today you will find the same division, and you will find that you still can get into some heated debates on the subject of the virgin birth.

The development of Roman Catholic doctrine in this particular area has meant controversy, because many Catholics who would hold very firmly to the doctrine find themselves opposed by many people who find it unacceptable. The Catholic theologians use with great enthusiasm a Greek word, *theotokos,* mother of God. This term made its way into theology many centuries ago at the time they were debating the deity and the humanity of Christ. And when Mary was talked about in this context, she was called the *theotokos* but as time went on, the emphasis moved away from her being the mother of *God* to her being the *mother* of God. The emphasis moved from Christology to Maryology.

At the same time, other aspects of Catholic dogma developed, too—the doctrine, of course, of the immaculate conception. So that I might state this properly, let me quote from a Catholic catechism for adults. This is what it says concerning the immaculate conception:

Christ alone is the redeemer of all. Mary, then, was redeemed by Him. He did not take away his mother's sins, for she had none. Rather, by his redemptive mercy he kept her from incurring sin so that she was conceived without original sin and was guarded by his grace against falling into sin.

People who do not adhere to Catholic dogma at that point would say, "There's no biblical basis for that whatsoever. That is purely a tradition given the weight of Scripture." At this point, Protestants and Catholics would take issue. Added to that is the teaching of the perpetual virginity of Mary. Catholicism has a wonderful Latin expression: *Ante partum . . . et post-partum*, which means that she was a virgin before the conception, during the birth, and forever after. People read their Bibles, so somebody will point out that Jesus had brothers and sisters. And the response is that they were probably brothers and sisters from a previous marriage of Joseph's, or the word could mean they were simply his cousins. At this point, there's considerable disagreement.

Then we get into the doctrine of the assumption of Mary, where she was presumed immune from the corruption of the tomb, ascended to the glory of heaven, and is now queen at the right hand of her son. This is Catholic tradition that has developed over the centuries and in relatively recent years—as late as 1950 for some of it—and become Catholic dogma. Many Protestants will simply look at all that and say, "That just ain't so. That is not what the Scriptures say," and they will feel that it paints Scripture as contradictory. So we see that the virgin birth is a hot button of controversy.

Implications of the Incarnation

How can we apply this? What are the implications of the Incarnation? The question that I've asked for many years is this, "Why was the virgin birth necessary? I believe it, but why was it necessary?" The answer I was given was that it was necessary to preserve the sinlessness of Christ. If he'd been born in the ordinary way, he would have been born with a sinful nature like the rest of us. That answer always bothered me. It seemed that, if that was the case, then sinlessness comes from your dad, and not from your mom. With all due respect to moms, they're wonderful, but they aren't perfect. So that didn't make any sense to me at all, that the sinlessness of Christ is preserved by the virgin birth.

Other people would say, No, the virgin birth was necessary in order to preserve the deity and the humanity of Christ. It couldn't have been done any other way. If he'd been born of two human parents, then he could not have been divine and human. Here again I don't see that that necessarily follows, but that answer is often given.

A more satisfactory answer that I find is that the point of the unique birth of the Lord Jesus is to alert us to the unique person of the Lord Jesus. As we are told of his unique birth, we put it in the back of our minds, don't worry about it too much, and then we look at him operating and we say to ourselves, *This is a unique person.* Then we say, *Oh yes, and the clue was given to us in the statement concerning the uniqueness of his birth.* What is this unique person? He is fully God, yet fully man, which means that he has come into our world to show us what God is like. If a little boy ever asked you, "Daddy, what is God like?" what would you answer? "Jesus." Jesus is fully God and yet fully man. But in his full manhood, Jesus reveals God in all his glory to us in a way that we can cope with, in a revelation that we can survive.

When there's an eclipse of the sun, you know as well as I do, you should never, ever look at the sun with your naked eye. You'll be blinded. If you want to look at the eclipse, you either look through smoked glass or you get a piece of paper, stick a hole in it, get the angle right, and get another piece of paper, and it will be projected onto the other piece of paper. But you never look directly at the unveiled glory of the sun.

So it is with God. God has revealed himself in Christ in such a way that we're not burned up by the revelation. He is fully God, revealed in a way that we can cope with. And therein lies one of the greatest implications of the Incarnation. It is God revealing himself in and through man. Not only that, but as he reveals God to us, he lives as fully man, yet without sin. This qualifies him as the spotless lamb of God who bore our sins in his own body on the tree. He did not die for his own sin. He was without sin. This was proved as he lived among us. As a man clearly observed by all, there was none who could bring any charge against him that was valid.

Therefore, we see in the unique birth a prefiguring of the unique person—fully God and fully human—revealing God to us and making it possible for us to be redeemed by a sinless sacrifice for sin. The unique birth also reminds us of a unique ministry. The unique ministry of the Lord Jesus down here on earth, among other things, is to show us how humans are to live. Here he is, fully God, yet fully man. And he shows how an ideal man, a perfect person, relates to the Father.

How does he do it? In ongoing obedience and total dependence. So as I look at the unique ministry of Christ, prefigured by his unique birth, what do I see? A unique person and a unique ministry that speaks to me about how I, as a human being, am supposed to relate to the Father.

The uniqueness of Christ also points to a unique model of how God works. Let me remind you of the little girl Mary. The angel says, "Mary, don't worry; be happy. A wonderful thing is going to happen to you. You found favor with God. Blessed are you among all people."

Mary says, "What's going on around here?"

The angel replies, "You're going to have a baby."

She says, "How can this be, since I don't know a man?"

And he says, "The power of the Holy Spirit will come upon you. You'll be overshadowed by the Holy Spirit."

Her response to that is, "Behold, the handmaiden of the Lord." (*Handmaiden* was simply a female word for a slave or a servant.) And then she says, "Be it unto me according to your word."

This is the model that Christ portrays to us to teach us the principle of divine blessing. The message comes to us through the appointed messenger. The good news comes that we have found grace with God, that he wants to move into our lives and over-shadow us with the power of the Holy Spirit. The news is his initiative; it is of him, of his grace, of his power. It is not of ourselves, but there's one thing that makes it possible. If the Holy Spirit was to come upon Mary, God wanted her glad acquiescence. If the power of the Spirit is to operate in my life in convicting and transforming, in revealing and opening my eyes and changing me, it requires my glad acquiescence.

So if a spiritual blessing is to ever come into my life, it will come because God in his grace has taken the initiative, told me what it is he will do, and has explained that it will be through the work of the Holy Spirit in my life. What is required for me to say is, "Behold the servant of the Lord; be it unto me according to your word." And that's what the virgin birth teaches us.

So when I say, "I believe in God the Father Almighty, maker of heaven and earth and in Jesus Christ his only Son, our Lord, who was conceived of the Holy Spirit, born of the virgin Mary," I'm making some powerful statements not only about my beliefs, but about how they impinge on my life, how they challenge me to live in this world, and the difference it makes in my life as opposed to that of the unbeliever.

We are privileged to believe. We are privileged to put what we believe into practical application. And we're privileged to live among men and women in such a way that our beliefs will take root in their lives and will be a help and a blessing to them. But it all depends what you believe, how thoroughly you believe it, and how the implications of it work out in your life.

MAKING IT PRACTICAL

1. What is our basis for belief in the virgin birth?

2. What are three ways of understanding prophecy?

3. What are some common objections to a literal understanding of the virgin birth?

4. What do we learn through the lives of Christ and Mary about how to relate to the Father?

6

"Suffered, Crucified, and Buried"

Luke 23:1-25

We're all familiar, I think, with the story of the betrayal of Christ by one of his intimates. We are not unaware of the trials he was subjected to that, in all probability, were totally illegal and were certainly unjust. We are not unaware of the fact that, even though he was found innocent, he was still punished by a flogging. We're aware of the fact that he was subjected to one of the most cruel executions ever devised by men, men who are capable of untold inhumanity to man. We're not unfamiliar with these things, but when we hear the story, we have a tremendous sense that this was an unmitigated tragedy. Most people agree that of all the men who ever lived Jesus Christ was the greatest. He came with blessing and goodness in mind. He devoted himself and he abandoned himself to other people, and yet he was betrayed, treated unjustly, and cruelly executed as a common criminal. It seems to be a tragedy of epic proportions.

It was a tragedy, that is, assuming he was just a man. But if we take this article of the creed in its context, if we take the statement of Christ's death in its biblical context, what we're talking about is not just a man dying tragically. We're talking about God assuming humanity and humbling himself to become a servant and being obedient even to death, even to death on the cross. We're talking about God being in Christ, reconciling the world to himself. And that is not tragic. That is a mystery of untold profundity, and we're stepping onto holy ground when we approach the sufferings of Christ.

Jesus' Suffering Before Pilate

When we think of Jesus suffering before Pontius Pilate, it is, I suppose, rather startling to us that these details should be included, and yet, apparently, it was important at the time this creed was put together. The writers focused on something that must continue to be our focus: the Cross of Christ. The central factor of Christianity is a cross, or, the crux of the matter is the Cross. In our modern language, we use the words *crux* and *crucial,* both of them from the Latin for cross. The Cross is crucial because it is the meeting point, the focal point of the Christian faith. It is a suffering Christ upon whom we focus our attention.

When we think of the sufferings of Christ, we tend to think primarily of his physical sufferings. I suppose when the Creed talks about him suffering before Pontius Pilate, it's talking about the inhumane flogging that he was subjected to immediately after he'd been declared innocent of any crime. When we study it more carefully, however, we'll discover that it's not particularly the physical sufferings that demand our attention.

Immediately prior to Jesus being brought before Pilate, the Roman procurator of Palestine, he'd been brought before the council of the elders, and the chief priests and teachers of the law were there. Jesus was brought before them, and they asked him if he was the Christ. He answered, "What's the point of telling you? You wouldn't believe me if I told you." Then they asked him specifically, "Are you the Son of God?" His answer was, "You said it." That may seem a little ambiguous to us, but there was no ambiguity as far as the people examining him were concerned, for their response was, "Why do we need any more testimony? We've heard it with our own ears."

The charge became blasphemy, and Jesus was subjected to phenomenal hostility by these ecclesiastical leaders. They challenged him on this claim to be Messiah, this claim to be the Son of God. They could not deny what he had done. They chose to deny who he was. There was tremendous hostility and antipathy towards him.

The interesting thing, however, is that if you check in Matthew 27:18, you'll discover that Pilate had a keen insight at this point. As he watched this council of elders, these teachers of the law, getting after Jesus and charging him with blasphemy, he saw inside these people. And this is what he saw: What was really upsetting them was envy. They were jealous of him. If you had asked one of those men, "Are you envious of Jesus?" they would have responded, "Of course not! It's a matter of principle; it's a matter of theology; it's a matter of blasphemy. That's what we're concerned about. It is truth and purity and integrity we're concerned about."

Pilate could see the truth, and he said, "Come off it! You're just jealous of him. He's showing you a clean pair of heels. He's done more in three years than you guys could do in a lifetime. He's set this place on its ear. All you have been doing is perpetuating a dead, dull, empty religious system. He's brought life. Come on, admit it." Jesus, of course, never needed to be told what was in a man either. One of the unnerving things about him is that he reads motives. And herein lies the suffering of Christ. He's being subjected to envy and jealousy cloaked in pious religiosity and ecclesiology. Therein lies the hurt.

I suppose all of us have had somebody envious of us for some reason at one time or another. But how often have we had other people come up to us and say, "I've got a problem. I've got to tell you something. I am so jealous of you. I hate your guts." How often do they do that? They don't say they're envious, and they don't say they're jealous. We know the hostility is there. We sense the antipathy, but they never really come clean about their real feelings.

The good thing about knowing that Jesus suffered is knowing the suffering Christ is an empathetic Christ. He is not unaware of what man does to man. He is touched with the feelings of our infirmities. Some of you are hurting because of the envious, jealous behavior of other people toward you, cloaked in all kinds of piety. The good news is that Christ understands. He suffered too.

They bring him before Pilate. On more than one occasion Pilate says that he is absolutely convinced of the innocence of this man. He says, "There is absolutely no charge for him to answer in my court. If you want to deal with him according to your laws, fine." In Palestine at that time, Roman law prevailed, and if anybody was to be executed, it was only under the signature of the Roman procurator. The leaders of the Jewish people at that time wanted him executed. They couldn't get him executed without getting Pilate to go along with it. Pilate said, "There's no charge to answer under my jurisdiction. If you want to get him on a lesser charge, you can handle it; go ahead, that's not my problem." When somebody suggested that he came from Galilee, Pilate shipped him off to Herod and said, "Maybe Herod can cope with it; he's in charge of Galilee."

Herod bounced him right back to Pilate. His wife said, "Don't have anything to do with this man," so he did the most asinine thing imaginable, which people still do today. He washed his hands of it. Knowing full well that he was simply a man, he as judge determined to have Jesus flogged and handed over to inevitable execution. He thought he could get away with it. He thought water and soap would rid him of his guilt. The gross injustice is unbelievable. Jesus Christ, who is righteousness personified, was subjected to that kind of injustice.

Some of you are hurting; you have been treated unjustly. You're resentful, and in some instances your resentment has coalesced into unrelenting bitterness. Yet we need to understand something: Jesus Christ knew the ultimate of injustice as he was subjected to untold emotional suffering by Pontius Pilate.

The dynamics between Herod and Pilate were interesting. Herod and Pilate had absolutely no time for each other at all. That was understandable. Herod was king of the Jews, and Pilate was in charge of Roman law and order. Pilate was a typical Roman governor, interested in keeping a firm hand on things, keeping a lid on the continual ferment of these Palestinian people. He was a heavy-handed sort of fellow. He did what he was going to do, and he didn't care about the consequences.

When he went to build an aqueduct, he misappropriated Jewish money for it. And when some of the Jews became livid about this and objected, he did the most abominable thing he could: He actually executed them at the place of their sacrifice and mingled the blood of the people he murdered with that of the sacrifices. This was an abomination to the Jewish religion. They utterly detested Pilate.

Herod was no great guy either. And Pilate despised him. But the most remarkable thing happened over this Jesus incident. Herod and Pilate, who hadn't had a good word to say about each other, became fast friends for political expediency. For it served both their purposes to get Jesus off their backs. And so they decided to put principle aside and do what was politically expedient and personally convenient. Therefore, Jesus became a victim of political expediency.

So are some of you. It was politically expedient in your business for you to be taken out of the way, and two people who had no time for each other in the hierarchy of your business got together to get rid of you. The good news, of course, is that as you're hurt, and as you're upset, and as you're being subjected to injustice, Jesus Christ, the suffering servant, at the crux of Christianity, stands with you in total empathy.

Some people have got the idea that God simply wound up the world and threw it into space and is sitting there twiddling his divine thumbs watching it wind down, trying to figure out how long it's going to take until the whole thing comes to entropy. Nothing could be further from the truth. He assumed our humanity, lived our life, and was hurt for our hurts, and that is the Christ of Christianity.

When Jesus is sent to Herod, Herod is greatly pleased, because for a long time he's wanted to see Jesus. He'd heard about the miracles that he did, and so he says to Jesus, "Do a miracle, would you? Just put on a miracle for me." And Jesus does the most unnerving thing; he just stands and looks at Herod and doesn't say anything.

A good friend of mine was talking about his father one day. His father is a very powerful person, a wonderful man. When this friend of mine was a boy and was in trouble with his dad, I sometimes acted as a go-between for these two because the dad was exactly as much older than me as I was older than his son. I was a close friend of both of them. So they both talked to me about this particular situation, and I said to the son, "What did your dad say?"

"Nothing."

I said, "What do you mean?"

"Nothing," he said, "he just . . ."

"What did he do?"

"He just looked at me."

"What did you do?"

He said, "I shriveled. I wished he'd say something. And in the end, I said, 'Dad, please say something! Don't just look at me.'"

And his father replied, "There's nothing to say."

I want you to picture Herod, shallow, superficial, standing before Jesus, who is basically saying to Herod, "I have nothing to say to you. You are longing for political expediency; you're out for number one; you don't care who goes to the wall; I have nothing to say to you."

Herod can't take this silence, and the ridicule and mockery and scorn and hatred burst out, and he joins with his soldiers in putting a purple robe on Jesus and slapping a crown of thorns on his head. They put a broken reed in his hand and mock his claims to be King of the Jews. Herod is the sort of person who's incapable of taking things seriously and can't handle somebody else who takes things seriously.

Some of you have that problem. You have tried very hard indeed, in the context of your family and workplace and friends, to get people to take being human very seriously. You've asked them to think seriously about issues of life and death. You've asked them to think about ethics and morality, and they just won't. Perhaps all they can do is give you shallow, superficial interest, and the only way they can cope is by mockery and ridicule, and you're hurt.

Therein lies the suffering of Christ. The suffering of Christ is that he knew what man was created to be, and yet he was subjected to what man had become. A few short days earlier they had welcomed him into Jerusalem shouting, clapping, and cheering, "The conquering hero comes! Hosanna in the highest! Blessed is he who comes in the name of the Lord." Now they're howling and screaming for his death. And he looks at them and he's saying, deep down in his heart, *I know what man was created to be and I see what man has become, and frankly, it breaks my heart.*

Some mothers have had great aspirations for their kids. They've seen the potential and they've seen what the kids did with that potential, and a sword has pierced their heart. Jesus, who is God assuming our humanity, who has made man in his own image, stands among the broken images of man that have fallen into utter degradation, and his heart breaks and suffers for humanity. Knowing who he is, knowing his intentions and motivations, knowing that he is the Way and the Truth and the Life, he realizes that they are telling him, "We don't want your way, and we don't want your truth, and we don't want your life. We don't want you." Therein lies the suffering of Christ, the utter and total rejection of one who came exclusively to bless.

One of my most vivid recollections of childhood in wartime England was sitting around a crackling radio with bombs dropping around us, shells going off above us, searchlights piercing the night sky, listening as hard as we could to the radio as the crackly voice of Winston Churchill told us we would never surrender. I read somewhere that after he'd given that highly motivating speech, he had put his head down on the table and burst into tears and said, "I don't know what we'll fight them with on the shores and on the beaches and in the streets, for we've nothing but beer bottles." For such was the power, the dynamism, the courage, and such would be the oratory of that man, that he made a besieged nation stand tall until her neighbors across the ocean came and joined hands.

A remarkable thing about the British people and Winston Churchill was that at the end of the war, there was an election. Churchill stood for re-election and was kicked out, a broken man. That is a picture in human terms of the sufferings of Christ. Knowing his commitment to righteousness, knowing his commitment to justice, and knowing his commitment to integrity, he doesn't see any righteousness, he doesn't get any justice, and nobody is interested in integrity. And therein lies his suffering.

I believe in Jesus Christ his only Son, our Lord, who was conceived by the Holy Spirit, born of the virgin Mary, suffered under Pontius Pilate and takes his stand with a bleeding, hurting, bruised humanity. He says, "I understand." What a tragedy it is, when you look at the major religions of the world, that people perceive God like their prophets, who stay removed. What a glorious thing it is to look at the uniqueness of Christ and see him assuming our humanity and bearing our sufferings.

Jesus' Suffering on the Cross

When you study the Gospel accounts of the death of Christ, it's interesting that the evangelists almost seem intent on drawing a veil over the details. Conversely, when we talk about the Cross, we usually focus on the physical sufferings. Though that's understandable, it's difficult for us to try and plumb the depths of the Cross, and therefore, the easier thing to do is simply to focus our attention on the physical agony and the bodily contortions of a crucified person. That is not inappropriate. But seeing the Bible says so little about it—in fact, the evangelists cryptically say, "And there they crucified him"—perhaps we should think harder. We should look more closely, see what is going on, as he suffers on the cross. There are two key words that help us understand the suffering of Christ.

Suffering through atonement

The first word is *atonement*. First John 4:9-10 gives us the key here. "This is how God showed his love among us: He sent his one and only Son into the world that we might live through him. This is love: not that we loved God, but that he loved us and sent his Son as an atoning sacrifice for our sins." Notice the expression "atoning sacrifice for our sins." It describes the atonement. Now what do we mean by the atonement? To understand that, we need to understand two things: the reality of the human condition and the intensity of the divine concern.

What is the human condition? The reality of the human condition is this: We don't love God. We love ourselves. That love for ourselves, as opposed to a love for God, has produced an independence of God and has degenerated into a rebellion against God. There's a simple monosyllabic word to describe this nonloving, independent, rebellious attitude toward God. In fact, it's an old-fashioned word that is rarely heard today: *sin*.

When our kids were growing up, they would engage in all kinds of peculiar behavior, as do all kids. When they were small, it was usually, according to their mother, either because they were tired or hungry or they had the flu or were teething. By the time they were eighteen, I felt they should have had all their teeth. By the amount of food they were putting away, I doubted very much if they could possibly be hungry. But you know what mothers are like; they always want to protect children from fathers. I used to ask a simple, and what I felt was an appropriate, question. When she would explain that they were hungry or tired or had the flu or were teething, I would ask, Couldn't it possibly be sin? And we came to the conclusion that possibly it could be sin. In anybody else's kid, it was obviously sin! But as far as ours were concerned, it could possibly be sin.

I want to ask the same question. We have developed many synonyms for sin. We have got a superb amount of data that

91

explains human behavior. We talk about nurture and nature: the nature that we're born with, our genetic makeup that makes us behave the way that we do; the nurture that we were subjected to, the environment into which we were born, the family of which we were a part, the things that happen to us. Because of our nature and because of our nurture, we have become the people we are. Behavior is explicable truly and simply in terms of nurture and nature. I disagree. Nurture certainly plays a part. Nature certainly plays a part. But sin plays a part too. If we don't deal with that, we don't deal either with the individual or with society, and we make the cross of Christ a sheer waste of time. He died as an atoning sacrifice for our sin. The mystery of the Cross is that in some way or other, the human condition of not loving God, being independent of God, rebelling against God, and releasing untold sin and evil in the world is being dealt with.

The Greek word that is translated "atoning sacrifice" here is *hilasmos*. It's a word that theologians have debated for decades, and here's the debate: Some say it means "propitiation," and others say it means "expiation."

Propitiation

Propitiation means doing something to appease or pacify someone's anger. A simple illustration: Jacob has ripped off Esau. Esau is ticked. Jacob splits. (You like *ticked* and *split* better than *propitiation* and *expiation,* don't you?) Eventually he has to come back home. He sends word, and he sends spies ahead to check out Esau. They come back. Esau is coming, and he is fit to be tied. Jacob gets presents and sends them to his brother, hoping to turn his frown into a smile. What is the Greek word, used in the Greek translation of the Old Testament for those gifts? *Hilasmoi.* He sends something to appease the anger of his injured brother.

Is the atoning sacrifice of Christ on the cross something to do with appeasing the anger of someone? If so, who? Romans chapter

3 tells us about this atoning sacrifice, this *hilasmos*. If you check the first three chapters of Romans, what is the dominant theme? The wrath of God. The simple thing we've got to get hold of is that the sin of man produces the wrath of God. And if man is ever to be reconciled to God, there needs to be a propitiation. There needs to be a dealing with the wrath, the anger, of God. At this point, we run into all kinds of rejection of the Christian gospel.

We will find what is commonly called the offense of the Cross. Someone might respond, "You don't mean to tell me that God is sitting up there throwing tantrums, being ticked, because we behave the way we behave when it's basically our nurture and our nature that makes us do it anyway? You believe in that kind of a God? And you mean to tell me that God took his perfect Son and stuck him on a cross and said, 'Okay, I feel better now?' You want me to believe that?"

That's the kind of thing you're going to come up against if you try to explain the Christian gospel to some people who have hold of one corner of it. They're assuming, of course, that the divine anger is like human anger. John Stott has a characteristic statement on this: "The wrath of God is his steady, unrelenting, unremitting, uncompromising antagonism to evil in all its forms and manifestations. In short, God's anger is poles apart from ours. What provokes our anger (injured vanity), never provokes his. What provokes his anger (evil), seldom provokes ours." The anger of God, the wrath of God, is the only response you can expect from a holy, righteous, just God against all that is unjust, untrue, impure.

The question is, How can a sinful humanity bear the wrath of God? Or how can God be appeased? Here's the mystery of the Cross: that God is the one whose anger needs to be appeased. God is the one who loves those who don't love, and God gives himself in Christ as a sacrifice for sin. He is the one whose love needs to be shown. He is the one who in Christ bears our sin, bears his wrath, and whose anger is appeased. There's the mystery of the Cross. He is bearing our sins in his own body on the tree.

Expiation

Not only that, he is the expiation for our sin. *Propitiation* means to appease anger. *Expiation* means to wash away sin, to make pure. I believe that Christ on the cross is a propitiation *and* an expiation. Dr. David Wells summarizes it beautifully for us:

> Man is alienated from God by sin, and God is alienated from man by wrath. It is by the substitutionary death of Christ that sin is overcome and wrath averted, so that God can look on man without displeasure and man can look on God without fear. Sin is expiated, and God is propitiated.

When we look at the Cross, we ask ourselves, Do I believe in substitutionary atonement? Christ died for our sins, mine included, so that God can look on me without displeasure and I can look on God without fear. He satisfies divine wrath and washes away sin as my substitute.

Notice the key word is *substitute*. When do we use the word *substitute?* When we give up sugar and we have a substitute, saccharine, a second-rate alternative. When do we use a substitute? When one of our starters gets injured and we put in one of our reserves. So when we think of a substitute, we think of a secondary alternative, or a reserve. Let me give you a better example. In an edition of our church's mission newspaper, there's a story of the Hmong people, whom we helped settle in Milwaukee and start their church. When they were coming out of their native country of Laos because of political and military pressure, they had to cross the river to get over into a haven. They knew that there were probably mines under the surface of the bank of the river, but they couldn't tell where they were, and they were afraid to go across. Then one of the old tribesmen came forward and said, "I'm an old man; I'll go first." And so the old man walked very carefully toward the bank of the river, one foot in front of the other, never knowing if next time he'd put his foot on a land mine. He did. He got killed. But the rest of them were able to come and put their feet where he'd put his feet, and they got across. Today they're leading a church in Milwaukee, Wisconsin, because of his substitutionary death.

Suffering through abandonment

The other word that helps me understand the suffering of the Cross is *abandonment*. While he was on the cross, Jesus suddenly cried out and the people misunderstood him. He cried out a quotation from Psalm 22:1, "My God, my God, why have you forsaken me?" And at that moment he cries out what is known technically as the cry of dereliction—the cry of abandonment.

I've been reading excerpts from a book by Nien Cheng, a Chinese woman in her fifties, called *Life and Death in Shanghai*. She was a widow of an oil executive who was trained in the West. She was captured by the Red Guard and accused of being a spy for the West for no other reason than she'd been educated in the West and was married to an oil executive, whose job she had held after his death.

They kept her in solitary confinement for six and a half years. They required her, under torture, to confess to being a spy. She refused on principle, so they handcuffed her hands behind her back and left the handcuffs on permanently. Her daughter was murdered by the guards while they were in prison.

They would bring food in to her, but her hands were handcuffed behind her back. She would put her face in her drink and lap up what she could like a dog. But how could she eat the food? She would put a rag on the floor, turn with her back to the table on which they placed the food, and with her manacled hands behind her, she would knock the food off the table onto the floor, hopefully onto the rag, and then get down like a dog and eat the food off the floor.

And this is what she said: "I never prayed, 'Oh Lord, get me out of this place.' I felt it was up to me to fight the battle, but the Lord would be with me. I could, through prayer, feel the Lord in the cell with me, so I never felt abandoned." That is one of the most incredible statements I've ever read.

Now, go to the Cross. If it is possible for somebody in solitary confinement, in those kinds of conditions, never to feel abandoned, because through prayer the presence of the Lord is felt, what must it be like, having been one with the Father for all eternity, suddenly to have your prayers hit a brassy heaven, and to cry from the depths of your soul, "My God, my God, why have you forsaken me?" The total emptiness of loneliness and abandonment is Christ suffering at that moment. And the answer comes—"for thou art holy." It's our sin—societal sin, corporate sin, national sin, international sin, and individual sin—that has separated Jesus and his God. Therein is the suffering of the Cross.

What do I believe about Jesus? Do I believe, as the writer of the Hebrews believed, that he tasted death for every man? Do I believe that he empathizes with suffering because he suffered as does every person? Do I believe that he propitiated my sin before a holy, righteous God? And do I believe that my sin is expiated because of his death? Do I believe this? The question is, Am I superficial like Herod or am I a coward like Pilate? Am I growing as I contemplate that Cross? Do I say to myself the words of the great hymn,

> When I survey the wondrous cross
> On which the Prince of glory died,
> My richest gain I count but loss
> And pour contempt on all my pride.
> Were the whole realm of nature mine
> That were an offering far too small,
> Love so amazing, so divine,
> Demands my soul, my life, my all.

MAKING IT PRACTICAL

1. What does atonement mean? What actually happens in the atonement?

2. What is the significance of Christ's cry of abandonment from the cross?

3. In our church and in our society, what has taken the place of sin in our vocabulary and in our thinking? What is the result?

4. What is your response to this consideration of the suffering of Christ?

7

"Rose Again from the Dead"

1 Corinthians 15:1-58

Ever since the Christian church came into being, there has been a solid insistence on the absolute necessity for the resurrection of Jesus Christ from the dead. The Resurrection has also been the main focus of attack from those who resist the Christian gospel. The apostle Paul was very aware of this resistance. Writing to the Corinthian church, he said that there were some of them who didn't believe that the dead would rise, and if the dead didn't rise, then Christ wasn't risen, and they must then consider the ramifications of wanting to be Christians who didn't have a risen Christ. He went on to show that if they truly believed that Christ was risen, then the result would be that they would stand firm, nothing would move them, they would always abound in the work of the Lord, and they would know that their lives were not being wasted. In other words, he talked about persistence through the Resurrection.

Insistence on the Resurrection

When we think in terms of the ministry of the early church, we've got to remember that the Lord Jesus gave instructions to a handful of people, and those instructions were absolutely phenomenal. They were simply to take the message of Jesus, starting in Jerusalem, to

Judea and Samaria and the uttermost parts of the earth. They set to work with a will. Quickly they embarked on the ministry in Jerusalem. Peter was the main spokesman, and his sermon on the day of Pentecost, the first Christian sermon, is recorded for us in the Acts of the Apostles. He concluded his sermon by saying this: "Therefore let all Israel be assured of this: God has made this Jesus, whom you crucified, both Lord and Christ" (Acts 1:36).

That was a decidedly dangerous and unpopular thing to say without this substantiation: God had raised him from the dead. That was the focal point of Peter's teaching and ministry, and he set the tone for the ministry of the early church.

In the Acts of the Apostles there are numerous accounts of various sermons that were preached and many people who made a defense of this one point, that Jesus Christ was risen from the dead. That was the focus point, and one that they insisted upon. They weren't just interested in evangelizing, letting people know some good news about Jesus. They were interested in making disciples out of these people, people who would learn about Christ and who would choose to follow him. So they embarked on their teaching.

When you look at their teaching, you'll find that a fundamental of that teaching was that Jesus Christ is Lord and they must acknowledge his lordship. But they had to give some undergirding to this statement that Jesus was Lord, and repeatedly they came back to the Resurrection, saying that, through it, God had shown that Jesus was Lord with all authority. They absolutely insisted in their preaching and in their teaching on the Resurrection.

As they were becoming more Christlike, the disciples knew that they would have different lifestyles. One of the characteristics of this new lifestyle is described for us by Paul as he wrote to the Colossians: "If you then be risen with Christ, seek those things which are above." So here we see that they're not only being taught that Christ was risen and that he was Lord, but that, in a very real sense, they had been raised with him to live a new life. The risen Christ took their attention away from purely human concerns and focused them on divine concerns. When they thought of the risen Christ seated in eternity at the Father's right hand, it took the focus of their attention away from time, into eternity, and away from earth to heaven. That began to be the dynamic of their new lifestyle. They were oriented differently.

Many men are oriented to purely human, secular, temporal, materialistic concerns. But those who became followers of the risen Lord were not so much concerned with worldly things, although they had their place. The dominant theme for them was divine, eternal, and spiritual. They had been raised with Christ, and the theme all along was the Resurrection.

Imagine these people, total strangers, moving into a new town, gathering the people in the marketplace, and saying, "Hey guys, I've got some great news for you. Jesus of Nazareth lived in Palestine a short time ago. He lived for thirty-three years. A wonderful, wonderful man. Born of a virgin, actually."

The people would respond, "Say, what?"

"Yeah, born of a virgin. He died on the cross for our sins."

"What?"

"Oh, yeah, and on the third day he rose again from the dead."

And the people said, "Sure! Yeah, sure! That kind of stuff happens here most days. Pigs fly, too!"

How in the world did they ever get anybody to take them seriously? How could they honestly go, as complete strangers, into a totally new town and get people to believe that Jesus was the Son of God? They argued the Resurrection, and they argued from historical data.

Let me remind you of this historical data: Jesus was crucified; some wealthy people asked if they could give him a decent burial and were given permission; they took the body down and put it in a tomb. Evidently it wasn't cared for as well as it might have been, and so some woman disciples decided they would come and care for the body properly. And when they got there, they discovered the stone was rolled away, the tomb was empty, and the body was gone. That was a historically verifiable piece of data.

101

The disciples who, without exception, had forsaken Christ out of fear at the time of his crucifixion, within three days were back together again—utterly transformed, totally different people. That is another piece of historical data.

The third piece of data is this: There were persistent reports and rumors that people had seen Jesus alive. Not just an individual, but large groups in several places over a period of time. In fact, on one occasion, up to five hundred people verified that they had seen the risen Lord.

"Now," said these disciples as they moved as total strangers into a new town and tried to get people to believe this ridiculous story that somebody had been raised from the dead, "You have got to accept the fact that there's a missing body, an empty tomb, some transformed disciples, and all kinds of reports and appearances. And we've got to have an explanation for them." That is still true today. People who believe in the resurrection of Jesus Christ are not engaging in wishful thinking; people who believe in the Resurrection are people who have looked at the evidence of the empty tomb, the missing body, the transformed disciples, and the reported appearances, and they have come to a conclusion as to an explanation of it.

There's another thing that we need to bear in mind. For some reason the church of Jesus Christ took root and flourished, even though the most unlikely people were given the responsibility for it. To illustrate this, here is a memo that I came across just a few days ago—a memo addressed to Jesus, son of Joseph, in the woodcrafter shop in Nazareth. It comes from the Jordan Management Consultants in Jerusalem, and the subject is A Staff Aptitude Evaluation:

Thank you for submitting the resumes of the twelve men you have picked for management positions in your new organization. All of them have now taken our battery of tests, and we have not only run the tests through our computers, but also have arranged personal interviews for each of them with our psychologists and vocational aptitude consultant. It is the staff opinion that most of your nominees are lacking in background, education, and vocational aptitude for the type of enterprise you are undertaking. They do not have a team concept. We would recommend that you continue your search for persons of experience in managerial ability and proven capability. Simon Peter is emotionally unstable and is given to fits of temper. Andrew has absolutely no qualities of leadership whatsoever. The two brothers, James and John, the sons of Zebedee, place personal interest above company loyalty. Thomas demonstrates a questioning attitude that would tend to undermine morale. We feel that it is also our duty to tell you that Matthew has been blacklisted by the Greater Jerusalem Better Business Bureau. James, the son of Alphaeus, and Thaddeus definitely have radical leanings, and they both registered a high score on the manic depressive scale. One of your candidates, however, shows great potential. He is a man of ability and resourcefulness, meets people well, has a keen business mind, and has contact in high places. He is highly motivated, ambitious, and innovative. We recommend Judas Iscariot as your controller and right-hand man. All other profiles are self explanatory. We wish you every success in your venture.

That points out in a very striking, dramatic way the total unsuitability of the disciples to do what Jesus told them to do. The embarrassing thing about it, however, is that they did it. How in the world do you account for it? How do you account for an empty tomb, a missing body, transformed disciples, reported appearances, and the sheer miracle of that church working? Well, these disciples raised questions and invited people to debate and discuss. Then they came up with their own explanation: God had raised up Christ from the dead; his disciples knew him and the power of his resurrection, and they would never, ever be the same again.

The question, of course, would come up, "Well, why would he raise him from the dead?" And three immediate answers come to my mind. First of all, to show his acceptance of Christ's passion. The death of Jesus Christ was either an unmitigated tragedy or it was an unbelievable victory, depending on your point of view. If Jesus was simply a good man who died a horrible death, it was an unmitigated tragedy. If, on the other hand, it was what he said it was, it was a supreme victory. Before his death Jesus said, "No man can take my life from me, I have power to lay it down and I have power to take it up again." He also said concerning his death, "I have come to give my life as a ransom for many." Either those statements were true or utterly, totally false.

By raising Christ from the dead, we believe that God reached down and said, in effect, "Son, I am with you. You're absolutely right, and I totally approve of all that you have done."

Then God looked at the world and said, "World, listen up a minute. You have done your worst with my Son. Now watch, and I will do my best." And he raised him from the dead. "World," says God, "that's what you think of my Son: you put him on a cross. Now watch; this is what I think of my Son." And he raised him from the dead.

Why did God raise him from the dead according to the apostolic preaching? It was to show that he accepted the death of Christ on our behalf. Secondly, he did it to demonstrate his divine power. There are many, many things that are terribly difficult for us in life. Often we wish that there was a power somewhere to help us stand firm, to overcome, to keep going. The biggest enemy, the Bible tells us, is death itself. Death is awesome and horrible, and death is something we cannot resist. It is an enemy.

We read lots of news as we're eating our meals, and it seems that the newspeople have a fixation on death. If it isn't a war somewhere, it's an airplane crash, a terrible accident on the freeway, somebody murdering somebody, or somebody drowning in an accident. It's always death. And we sit there and it grips us because it bothers us, because there's nothing we can do about it. Then it strikes home to our own hearts.

Thirty years ago now, I got a phone call from my brother, and what he said was utterly shattering: "I don't know how to tell you this, but Dad's dead."

I said, "What?"

"Dad's dead."

I was torn up. He said Dad was talking to mother, and he took a deep breath and was gone. He was dead. I'll never forget the icy feeling I felt at that moment. I jumped in the car with Jill, who at that time was about eight months pregnant with our first child, and we drove to my mother's. My mother was a self-possessed woman, very capable, very strong. I'll never forget her reaction as I got out of the car: she grabbed me and said, "What are we going to do? What can we do? What am I going to do?" She was shaken. That icy feeling hadn't left me. She was totally unnerved. I entered the room where my father's body lay, and he was very, very dead. I realized that there was something irresistible and irrevocable about death. You know that, too. What a dreadful thing it is to realize that's where we're all heading.

But the question is, Is that dreadful enemy going to win in the end? And the answer is, If you believe in the Resurrection, no. For when God raised Christ from the dead, he demonstrated his mighty power to be greater than our greatest enemy. He did it to put his seal of approval on Christ's passion, to demonstrate his mighty power, and to fulfill his eternal purpose.

God's purpose was to create a universe and a humanity with which he could have intimacy of fellowship. Humanity decided to thwart the divine purpose by abusing its God-given free will. The result was a humanity cast adrift from God. God was not through with humanity. His eternal purpose had not changed—to enjoy intimacy with humanity. So he took the initiative and in the Incarnation, sent his Son. In the Crucifixion, his Son bore the consequences of our sin so the barrier between humans and God might be removed. In the Resurrection he defeated death. And in the Ascension he opened a way into the presence of God. So the eternal purpose of God required incarnation, crucifixion, resurrection, and ascension to bring an estranged humanity back into relationship with God. The eternal purposes of God required the Resurrection. The insistence of the early church on the Resurrection was easy to understand, for everything hinged on that.

Can you stand tall and say, "I believe that on the third day he rose again from the dead?" Can you insist on it? For if you do, you will have already found out that there are people who resist that idea. They certainly did in Corinth when Paul was teaching there, and they do in our world today.

Resistance to the Resurrection

Let me identify three points of resistance that we may or may not have come across. There is the resistance of the rationalist. The rationalist puts it this way: "You Christians say that a dead man rose again. Any dummy knows that dead men don't rise again. Therefore, we arrive at one of two conclusions about you Christians. Either Jesus wasn't dead when you say he was, or you're lying through your teeth." And that is the situation we confront when we endeavor to share the message of the risen Christ with our secular world.

Presuppositions of the naturalist

What do we do about it? Well, we don't get into a big debate as to whether he did or whether he didn't, because that's probably going to be futile. What we do is get back to presuppositions. The presupposition of the rationalist is that our world is a self-contained entity running on laws and rules and principles that are never violated. That being the case, there is a rule and a principle in our world, that when you die you stay dead. Period. So if your presupposition is that our world is a closed system, operating on its known laws, you have no alternative than to believe that dead men don't rise, and Jesus, therefore, didn't rise from the dead.

There's another presupposition, however: that our world was created by God, that he put it into operation, and he established the laws and the rules and the principles. He reserves the right and has the divine prerogative to intervene if he so desires. A miracle is a divine intervention into the world that he created and an exercise of his prerogative which no human being has the right to deny him.

So it comes down to this: Either my presupposition is that the world just happened and is a closed system, or my presupposition is that God created it, put the laws in operation, and reserves his divine right to intervene as and when he wishes. The Resurrection is a divine intervention. It is the divine prerogative being exercised, and who among human beings can deny God the right to do that? Let them stand up and be counted.

Resurrection or reincarnation?

Another kind of resistance that we'll come across is not so much from the rationalist, but from the reincarnationalist. Some of the advocates of reincarnation in the New Age movement are trying to show that when the Bible talks about resurrection, what it really means is reincarnation. This is despite the fact that the Bible says it is appointed unto man once to die and after that the judgment.

The ancient Greeks believed in reincarnation, at least some of them did, but we are most familiar with reincarnation theory in the eastern religions like Hinduism. The Hindus believe in the transmigration of the soul. By transmigration they mean that souls need bodies to live in, and they inhabit the body until the body dies, and then the soul simply migrates to another body. If your karma has been good, the result is that your soul, having abandoned its dead body, finds a better one as a reward for good karma. If you do a good job there, then the next time your body dies, your soul transmigrates to another, better situation until in the end you arrive at enlightenment. You arrive at purity. You are absorbed into the total cosmic oneness.

The other side to Hindu reincarnational thinking is that if your karma is bad, then your soul migrates to a lesser form of life, a lesser body. It could even move into an animal's body. That is why the Hindu is a vegetarian, for very obvious reasons. No one wants to eat Grandma. And let's face it, if I honestly, genuinely believed that when my grandmother died her soul left her body—and because she was a mean old girl, she came back as a cow—then clearly I'm going to be very careful.

Western people have taken the part of reincarnation they want and carefully ignored the rest. The bit they've taken is the good karma, and they have ignored the bad karma. So in New Age thinking now, Shirley MacLaine, et. al., are saying that what really happens is that when you die you don't face the judgment and the resurrection. Instead, your soul simply migrates better and better and better until you merge with the cosmic oneness. One of those is wrong. For you see, reincarnation is the migration of the soul, but resurrection is divine intervention in mortality, transforming it into immortality. So, when you stand up tall in your society today and you meet a delightful New Age person who probably isn't thinking too clearly on this point, challenge him on what he really believes, whether it's reincarnation or resurrection.

The revisionist approach

Another point of resistance to the idea of the Resurrection is what I would call the *revisionist approach*. That is where people sort of have lip service to the idea of resurrection but can't go all the way with it. Harvey Cox, a professor at Harvard Divinity School, said, "We will have to live the rest of our lives both with the affirmation that in some way Christ lives among us and with the gnawing doubt that this really isn't possible." So in other words, what we've got to do somehow or another is believe what we know is totally unbelievable. Those sorts of people would say there's no question about it that those early disciples really believed Jesus was risen from the dead (He clearly wasn't, because dead men don't rise), but it was good for them, it helped them, and they got their church started—and faith is a wonderful thing. "Keep the faith, brothers." (When you ask them which one, they're not sure.) But you'll find this type of resistance to the Resurrection.

Writing to the Corinthians, Paul says that if you reject the Resurrection, you've got to be clear about the ramifications. First Corinthians 15:13-19 says,

> If there is no resurrection of the dead, then not even Christ has been raised. And if Christ has not been raised, our preaching is useless and so is your faith. More than that, we are then found to be false witnesses about God, for we have testified about God that he raised Christ from the dead. But he did not raise him if in fact the dead are not raised. For if the dead are not raised, then Christ has not been raised either. And if Christ has not been raised, your faith is futile; you are still in your sins. Then those also who have fallen asleep in Christ are lost. If only for this life we have hope in Christ, we are to be pitied more than all men.

If Christ is not risen, says Paul, the Christian message is fatally flawed, Christian faith is utterly without foundation, and all Christian witness is false. If Christ is not risen, Christian forgiveness is a total fallacy. If Christ is not risen, Christian burial is a sham. When we bury somebody, we commit their remains to the ground. Earth to earth, dust to dust, ashes to ashes, *in sure and certain hope of the resurrection.* And that is the biggest hoax; that is the most merciless and cruel flim-flam ever perpetrated on anybody if it isn't true. The biggest hucksters, the biggest rascals in the world are ministers of religion who tell grieving people, when the remains of their loved ones are laid to rest, that there's a resurrection. If that isn't true, the whole thing is an unspeakable hoax, and they all should be locked up. And if Christ is not risen, Christian hope is utterly futile. So we see we're pushed into a corner on this resurrection thing. And we have to decide what we believe.

Persistence through the Resurrection

What's the practicality of this for you? The apostle Paul says in 1 Corinthians 15:32, "If I fought wild beasts in Ephesus for merely human reasons, what have I gained? If the dead are not raised, 'Let us eat and drink, for tomorrow we die.'" His point is this: Hey, you guys, I want you to realize something. I'm going around this planet preaching that Jesus is raised from the dead, making disciples. People are beating me up. I've been shipwrecked. I've been starving. In Ephesus I've fought wild beasts. (We don't know whether they were literal wild beasts or people behaving like wild beasts.) He said, Hey, who needs it? I can go back to making tents; I made a nice living. If Christ is not raised from the dead and I'm doing all this stuff, I am the biggest dummy you ever saw. If Christ is not raised, why would I spend my time doing this? I may as well join those Epicureans who say, "Let us eat and drink for tomorrow we die." Our culture has a slight variation on that theme now: "You only go around once in life; hit it with all the gusto you've got." That is American Epicureanism.

Here are our options: If Christ is not risen, please put up the shutters of my church and close down all these wretched churches. Get these people off the radio and television. Make people like me go back to earning an honest living. Stop this whole charade. Quit the whole business. But listen, if you tell me that Christ isn't risen, I'm going to be an epicurean too. I'm going to hit it with all the gusto I've got. If there's nothing after this and this is all we've got, let's get out there and live it up.

If, on the other hand, he is risen, the world needs to know, and I need to live as if he is. If I'm raised with Christ, I need to set my mind on things above. I'm going to have to decide which way I'm going to go. And then I'm going to have to persist. This is how Paul concludes: "Therefore, my dear brothers [including sisters], stand firm, let nothing move you, always give yourselves fully to the work of the Lord, because you know that your labor in the Lord is not in vain." What he is saying is, Wild beasts, look out; I'm not through with you yet. I'm going to keep going because Christ is risen. I'm going to stand firm; I won't budge; I'll keep going because we're going to win.

I believe in God the Father Almighty,
Maker of heaven and earth;
And in Jesus Christ his only Son our Lord;
who was conceived by the Holy Spirit,
born of the Virgin Mary,
suffered under Pontius Pilate,
was crucified, dead, and buried,
and descended into Hades.
The third day he rose again from the dead.

I believe it with all my heart; therefore, I'm going to stand firm. Therefore, I'm not going to budge. Therefore, I'm going to keep going until I drop. You know why, don't you? Because if Jesus Christ is risen, that's where the action is.

MAKING IT PRACTICAL

1. What is the importance of the Resurrection?

2. What are three strong pieces of evidence for the Resurrection?

3. Describe three groups of people who resist the idea of Christ's literal resurrection from the dead.

4. What is it that bothers us so much about death?

5. What are some of the practical implications of the Resurrection? If Christ did rise, what should our lives be like?

8

"He Ascended into Heaven"

Ephesians 4:1-6;
Philippians 2:5-11

Recently *Newsweek* magazine did a special issue on what people think about heaven. Seventy-seven percent of people in the United States believe that there is a heaven. Seventy-six percent believe they have a good or excellent chance of getting there. Fifty-eight percent of them, however, believe in hell, and only 6 percent of them think that they have a good or excellent chance of getting there.

When they were asked what they thought heaven might be like, 91 percent thought it would be peaceful, 83 percent thought they would be with God, 77 percent thought they will see people they know, 74 percent thought there will be humor, and 32 percent thought they will be the same age in heaven as when they die on earth.

Do you believe in heaven? What do you believe about it? Andrew Greeley, a Roman Catholic priest, sociologist, and novelist, has done a lot of research in this area. And he says that most Americans regard heaven as being a continuation of life on earth but without the wars, diseases, and other inconveniences that cramp their present pursuit of happiness. Notice the expression "pursuit of happiness."

He himself admits to having been hypnotized so that he could discover what his subconscious views of heaven were, and he discovered that from his subconscious emerged an image of heaven as like an emerald city on a lake. As he approached, it turned out to be his hometown, Chicago! This may have turned some of you off on heaven immediately!

He points out that most people's perception of heaven is that it is like all the good things on earth, with all the bad things taken out, and just sort of hyped up a bit. So healthy and wealthy people imagine a sort of celestial Caribbean island with an endless blue horizon and loved ones whispering, "It doesn't get better than this!"

But those who work in hospitals have noticed that for aged and terminally ill people, heaven is a place of release from all that ails them. There's a rather poignant statement here concerning pediatric cancer patients. They believe that heaven is a place where they will no longer have to listen to Mom and Dad cry and fight, a place where they won't have to come to the hospital for chemotherapy treatments anymore. AIDS patients regard heaven as freedom from pain. Elderly people regard it as a place of ultimate rest because they are so tired. But they have mixed feelings about it because they are afraid of being lonely there; there may not be people they know.

And so, the vast majority of the people in the United States believe in heaven, and their perceptions of heaven are basically that it is sort of a celestial United States of America with all the really nice things improved and all the nasty things taken away.

Of course, some people have problems with the statement "He ascended into heaven." They say this perception comes from the old days, in which the idea was that there was a tiered universe, that earth was the center, and then under earth was the underworld. And then above that was heaven, in seven tiers, so it was possible to go to the seventh heaven. But then we started space travel and began to discover that our universe is somewhat different. So the idea of ascending into heaven becomes problematic for some people.

If you ascend from the United States and ascend from Australia, of course, you're moving in totally opposite directions. And so the question for many people is, Well, is heaven a place, or is heaven a state? And people are not always prepared to deal with that.

It's interesting to notice the ambivalence that many people have towards heaven. They believe in it, but they're not too sure about how soon they want to get there. You probably heard about the two fellows who were talking, and one of them said to the other one, "I've got some good news and some bad news for you."

The second fellow responded, "Okay, give me the good news first."

The first fellow said, "The good news is that yes, there's baseball in heaven, and you made the team."

"Well," the other said, "that's great; what's the bad news?"

And the first fellow replied, "The bad news is, you're the starting pitcher tomorrow morning."

This points out the ambivalence that people have about heaven. It's something wonderful, but they don't want to go there too quickly, because most of them are having a pretty good time on earth.

There's considerable confusion and ambivalence, even though there's general belief in heaven. Of course the Christian affirms, with tremendous confidence, belief in Christ, who "ascended into Heaven and sitteth on the right hand of God the Father Almighty." But what do we mean by this? Let me identify three things for you: First of all, I want to remind you of what the ascension of the risen Lord means; second, to show you that the idea of him sitting at the right hand of God the Father speaks of the authority of the risen Lord; third, to conclude by talking about the activity of the risen Lord. What is he doing in glory at the present time?

Christ's Ascension

When I was a boy in England, one of the books I was required to study in English Literature, which was my favorite subject, was Kinglake's *Eothen*. King Lake traveled all over the East and wrote a terribly boring book about it. We knew it had to be great literature because it was so boring. I've been to the East many times, and I can't understand how anybody could write such a boring book about it!

Travelogues are very popular. Those of you who come from Germany probably were reared on the stories of the travels of Seigfried. And if you weren't, you listened to Wagner's operas based on them. Those of you who had a classical education are familiar with Homer's *Iliad* and stories of the great travels that came at the end of the Trojan War as Hector began to find his way home. People have always been interested in human beings engaging in great journeys.

The ascension of Jesus Christ is an integral part of the greatest journey that anybody ever made. Let me trace that journey for you, from Philippians 2, where we have an ancient hymn that recounts this journey. This is what it says about Christ:

> Being in very nature God, [he] did not consider equality with God something to be grasped, but made himself nothing, taking the very nature of a servant, being made in human likeness. And being found in appearance as a man, he humbled himself and became obedient to death—even death on a cross! Therefore God exalted him to the highest place and gave him the name that is above every name, that at the name of Jesus every knee should bow, in heaven and on earth and under the earth, and every tongue confess that Jesus Christ is Lord, to the glory of God the Father.

Notice, first of all, that there are two stages in this great journey of Christ. The first stage is his descent. The second stage is his ascent. Notice that Christ started off with glorification. The Scriptures tell us that before the worlds were created, he shared in the glory of the Father. He was equal with the Father. But when the call came for him to deal with the redemption of the human race, he did not regard this glory and his equality as something to be held on to. He was prepared to divest himself of it and go on the second stage of his journey from glorification to incarnation.

In the Incarnation, Christ empties himself of all the trappings and prerogatives of deity. He does not cease to be deity, but he applies to himself, he assumes to himself, our humanity. Laying aside his glory, assuming our humanity, he accepts all the limitations of life as man among men.

The third stage of his journey is his humiliation. He accepts anonymity. He is born in the back of nowhere. He is part of a family that nobody particularly knows. He accepts humanity. He accepts anonymity. He even humbles himself to the point of becoming a servant.

The fourth stage in his journey is crucifixion. He submits himself to death, the most heinous of all possible deaths, the death of the cross, and he endures the torment of crucifixion. And according to the Apostles' Creed, he descends into Hades (or descends into hell, depending on which version of it you use). People are confused at this point as to whether it is hell or Hades, and the confusion is somewhat understandable.

Hades is a Greek word that is equivalent to the Hebrew word *Sheol*. And *Sheol* can just mean the grave, or it can be applied to the realm of departed spirits. There is another word, *Gehenna,* which related to a valley where the refuse was burned outside Jerusalem, an awesome, dreadful place that was often taken as a picture of hell.

Sometimes the words are used interchangeably, and when Scripture tells us, "You will not leave his soul in hell," the theme here is Hades rather than Gehenna. And so some people have used the old word *hell;* others prefer to use the word *Hades.* But, having said that, there is considerable difference of opinion as to what Hades is. Some say it is simply the grave; others say, no, it is a realm where the departed spirits await the great resurrection.

Some people say that Hades has two sections to it. You remember the dying thief was told by the crucified Lord, "Today you will be with me in paradise"? If Christ descended into Hades that day and met the dead thief there and said it was Hades, they say presumably that half of Hades is paradise and half of Hades is the waiting room for the other place. We cannot be dogmatic about this, but what we can say is that the journey of our Lord Jesus went from glorification, to incarnation, to humiliation, to crucifixion and all that death entailed. But from that point on, his journey moves into ascension. The next state was his resurrection. "God exalted him to the highest place and gave him the name that is above every name."

The resurrection was the divine seal of approval on what he had accomplished, and the sign of his great victory. But it was not complete yet. For then he ascended into heaven and was given the highest place and the greatest title. Imagine all the wonderful places, the place of authority, the place of opportunity, the place of responsibility, that are Christ's through his ascension, through his resurrection. Imagine all the great titles; imagine all the great names that belong to Christ in his ascension.

The day is coming, however, when the ascended Lord will receive the glory that is his due. There is a day coming, Paul tells us, when every knee will bow to him and every tongue will confess that Jesus Christ is Lord. And that will be the conclusion of his journey, a great circular journey from glorification to incarnation, to humiliation, to crucifixion, to resurrection, to ascension, to the ultimate glorification.

When we look at it in that light, we can see how the often-neglected ascension of Christ is absolutely crucial. It would have been unthinkable to have a Christ who was simply incarnated. It would be dreadful to think of a Christ who was simply crucified. If Christ had simply been raised from the dead and stayed around here and died a natural death, that wouldn't have been very helpful either. His ascension was vital, and his ultimate glorification restores him to the place that he had before he accepted responsibility for our redemption. And so we affirm that we believe in Jesus Christ who ascended into heaven and is seated at the right hand of God the Father Almighty.

Christ's Authority

What does it mean that Christ is at the right hand of God the Father Almighty? This speaks of his authority. And the picture of him sitting at God's right hand, the place of greatest privilege and the place of greatest authority, is very dramatic. But there are other pictures as well. Hebrews 1:13 quotes Psalm 68 and tells us that Christ in glory right now is waiting until his enemies be made his footstool. Ancient conquerors, to demonstrate their total triumph over their vanquished foes, would prostrate them before them and then put their feet on their necks. Here you have a picture of all the enemies of God and all the enemies of Christ being required to be prostrated before Christ and become his footstool.

The believer who confesses belief in the ascension of Christ and him sitting at the right hand of God is really saying, "I believe Christ is glorified as he ought to be for the work that he has done, because of his character, and because of his nature, but I also believe that he has ultimate authority, that all his enemies will be subdued by him." This is good news for believers, because all his enemies are our enemies too. Think of sin. Think of death. Think of hell. Think of Satan. Think of all the evil you can and realize it's only a matter of time until all these things line up as his footstool when his ultimate, final, irrevocable and universal triumph is seen by all. And at that point, every mouth will confess he truly is Lord and every knee will bow and confess his lordship. That is the picture being conveyed of his authority.

Ephesians 4:8 gives us another picture, quoting, or, some people would say, misquoting Psalm 110. Paul says, "When he ascended on high, he led captives in his train and gave gifts to men." The reason some people say he misquoted it is that in Psalm 110 the idea is of the ascending victor receiving gifts from men. And so some people, rather skeptical of Paul, said, "He just altered this to make it fit his presuppositions." That's hardly fair.

119

You see, the situation was this: When kings would return in triumph from their victories, they would receive gifts from those they had conquered. But they would immediately take these gifts and distribute them to the people who had helped gain the victory. As they came back into their capital city, they would chain representative prisoners behind their chariots.

You say, Why would they do that? Today, if our leaders want to give us an idea of what's happening in a war right now, they send intrepid photographers and intrepid soundmen and reporters out into the midst of the battle, and there they capture the sounds and the sights for us that we can watch while we have our breakfast. Then we know what the war is all about. But in the ancient days, they couldn't do that, and so they would bring evidences of the victory and parade them through the city. The expression "leading captives in his train" is simply portraying that image for us. Christ is leading captive all the things that contributed to his seeming defeat on the cross and his descent into death. He bursts out through these things and leads them, clearly conquered by him—another picture of his authority.

Notice also, in Colossians 2, yet another picture of his authority. It says in verse 15, "And having disarmed the powers and authorities, he made a public spectacle of them, triumphing over them by the Cross." Christ has disarmed all the powers, all the authorities, all the forces that oppose God and his Christ and that have such a detrimental effect on society and individuals. Think of all the things that contribute to the evil in the world. Christ, through his death and resurrection, has disarmed them. The Greek word translated "disarmed" means literally to strip away. So he could mean that he took all these offensive powers and conquered them and stripped away from them all their armaments, or it can mean that these forces overwhelmed him and he threw them off; he stripped them away. Either way, they are powerful pictures of the great victory and power and authority of Christ.

So, when we say we believe in Christ ascending into heaven and sitting at the right hand of God the Father Almighty, we're talking about his glorification and his place of ultimate, final, irrevocable authority. His authority in practice means that he is in charge of all powers. It means that he has a title greater than all titles. It means that he is Generalissimo, supreme, *numero uno*.

David Thorson, an English preacher, makes this point well: "This is God's world, and he wants it back, and he's told us to get it for him." I find that very invigorating. But you see, I meet a lot of people who don't believe this is God's world, so they have no concept of him wanting it back. They're not remotely interested in being involved in getting it back for him.

The question I want to ask you is this: When you say that you believe that Christ ascended into heaven and is seated at the right hand of God the Father Almighty, whose world do you believe this is? Do you believe that his is the ultimate authority, that it is his world? If so, it's in a shambles, and he wants it back. The question is, Who's going to get it for him? And the answer is that he is not only over all powers and over all authorities, but he is the head of the church, and the church is to be the medium through which Christ gets his world back.

Immediately this becomes essentially practical. Suddenly I'm not simply reciting a dull creed; I am capturing the excitement of what it means to believe that I am part of the church of which Christ is the head. The church's function is, under his headship, to be the means of getting his world back for him so that his authority can be clearly demonstrated and his glory acknowledged.

Unfortunately, our concept of the church is often considerably lower than that. The church seems to be what we call "our church." I hear people talking about "our church," and "our church" this and "our church" that and then they talk about "your church." People come up to me when I'm traveling and say, "Tell us about your church; what's happening in your church?" I cringe when I hear people say, "Oh, we visited Milwaukee and we went to Stuart Briscoe's church." It absolutely, emphatically is not mine, and I don't want it; it's his. You see, if it was mine, it would be mine to direct and mine to control and mine to govern. And if it was yours, it would be yours to direct and yours to govern and yours to simply do what you want it to do. But it isn't mine, it isn't yours, and it isn't anybody else's. It's his. And he, seated at the right hand of the Father, with ultimate authority committed to him, with this world his by right, wants it back; he is bent on getting his church to be the means of getting it back for him. That's what we're all about.

So when we think in terms of the ascended Lord, we begin to think of something essentially practical, powerful, and exciting in our lives.

Christ's Activity

But what is it that he's doing now? When we begin to think in terms of what the church is intended to be under his headship, it's encouraging to hear that one of the things he's doing is sending his Spirit into the world. The apostle Peter, in his Pentecostal sermon recorded in Acts 2:33, says, "Exalted to the right hand of God, [Christ] has received from the Father the promised Holy Spirit and has poured out what you now see and hear."

What is the point of this? One of the points of him sending his Spirit into the world is that the Holy Spirit is the dynamic that equates to all the demands of God. Let me explain what I mean by that. God has laid great demands on individual Christians and on the corporate body of believers, the church. And we are totally overwhelmed by the immensity of these demands. We can't live the way we're supposed to live. The church can't be what it's supposed to be. We're a bunch of sinners, and the church is made up exclusively of sinners. How can we possibly do all that he demands of us? And the answer is, through the Holy Spirit. God doesn't just make demands on us; he sends his Spirit, and he begins to empower individual believers and the corporate whole. So whenever you see a Christian who professes to believe in the Christ who's ascended and seated at the Father's right hand, you can expect to see a powerful Christian—empowered by the Spirit the ascended Lord is sending to his or her life.

We also noted, in Ephesians 4, that he is granting gifts to his people. So his church, empowered by the Holy Spirit, is made up of people with gifts—spiritual abilities that the Holy Spirit gives, through Christ, to every believer. And each gifted person then becomes God's gift to the world through the church.

One day a reporter from one of the Milwaukee papers came to see me after three Sunday morning services at Elmbrook. Now when I am through after three Sunday morning services, all I want to do is get away and eat. People say, "You must be exhausted!" I say, "I'm not exhausted, just hungry." I work up an appetite. This particular reporter wanted to talk to me. I'd seen him climbing over people, taking pictures, and I didn't particularly want to talk to him. He hadn't asked for an appointment or anything.

I was standing down in the front. He came walking down that aisle and, about halfway down, shouted to me, "Would you say you're gifted?"

I said, "What?"

He said, "Would you say you're gifted?"

I said, "Yes."

He said, "I think you're arrogant."

"Well," I said, "I think you're ignorant." Okay, time out. This wasn't a very good start to our conversation. Then I said, "I assume that the reason you think I'm arrogant is that when you asked me if I was gifted, I didn't say, 'Oh, shucks, no. No, I'm just an ordinary sort of guy, no, no.' But I didn't say that, I simply answered in the affirmative—yes, I think I'm gifted. Now, I can understand why you thought I was arrogant. Let me explain to you why I know you're ignorant. The Bible says that every believer is gifted. So there's no way I could answer any other way than yes. So I'm not arrogant; I'm just telling you the truth. But you didn't know that. That's why you're ignorant. But the good news is this, you're not ignorant anymore, because now you know never to ask that question again of a believer, because every believer is gifted."

How about you? Are you ignorant? You see, the ascended Lord is sending his spirit and granting his gifts. And he's gifting every believer so that he or she becomes a precious resource for the church. And that precious gift to the church is involved in bringing the church to maturity, helping it to grow, and equipping everybody to do the work of ministry. So ultimately believers, gifted by the risen Lord, give to the church and become a gift to the world, and that's you and that's me. So if you're worried about being ignorant, don't worry—you're not anymore. You're very, very knowledgeable!

The big question is this: Have you discovered where, how, when, and why in the power of the Holy Spirit to exercise the gifts that God has given you in the church, for the good of the world, for the glory of Christ?

Thirdly, and finally, he is representing the redeemed. In Romans 8:34, Paul says, "Who is he that condemns? Christ Jesus, who died—more than that, who was raised to life—is at the right hand of God and is also interceding for us." There's a great question here: Who is going to condemn Christians? And the answer is, lots of people. Do you ever get criticized? No! Do I ever get criticized? No! Do people ever give you or me a hard time because of what we do? No! Everybody pats us on the back all the time, right? Wrong! There are all kinds of people who will take every opportunity to point out all our failures and all our faults.

But the good news is this: Seated at the Father's right hand is a personal representative of all the redeemed. And he makes intercession for you, he speaks well of you, and he represents you well to the Father. This is wonderful news! You see, some of you feel lonely. Some of you feel rejected. Some of you feel that life is such a burden. Some of you wonder if it's worth going on—nobody seems to care whether you live or die. You couldn't be more wrong.

For there is, at the Father's right hand, a representative of all the redeemed. He shows in his glorified humanity the wounds of the Cross, which speak of your redemption. In exactly the same way that the Holy Spirit is God the Father's advocate to us, so the risen Christ is our advocate to the Father.

You have a representative in Washington. You've probably never seen him. If you have seen him, you've probably never talked to him. If you talked to him, he probably didn't take any notice of you. He was elected, and he will be there until they elect somebody else in his place. The representative of the redeemed, who is in the immediate presence of the Father, was not elected; he is there by divine right. He has completed his glorified journey. He reigns and rules with the ultimate authority. He sends his spirit. He grants his gifts. He represents you before the Father. He is the ascended, glorified, totally authoritative Lord!

MAKING IT PRACTICAL

1. Describe Christ's "journey" recorded in Philippians 2:5-11. What does it mean that he "ascended"?

2. What are three of the things Christ is presently doing in our world?

3. What is the significance of the outcome of the survey that showed that 77 percent of Americans believe there's a heaven, and 76 percent believe they have a "good to excellent chance" of getting there, while only 58 percent believe in hell, and only 6 percent believe they have a "good to excellent chance" of getting there? What does that say about our society and our self-perception?

4. How do you respond to David Thorson's statement that "This is God's world, and he wants it back, and he's told us to get it for him"?

9

"He Shall Come"

John 14:1-3

People have always been fascinated with the idea of the world coming to an end. There are some people who are optimistic; they have decided in relatively recent years that the world is infinite, that it had no beginning and it will have no end. They believe the world will just continue existing and that the infinite universe, as we know it, is the sum totality of all reality. But other people, and probably the majority, feel that that isn't quite how it's going to be. They sense that this world of ours is winding down.

Not infrequently, we're told all kinds of gloomy things concerning the condition of our world. We're told about holes being burned in the ozone layer and the possibility of the ozone being gradually destroyed until in the end the rays that are so destructive to us will not be kept out and we'll all be shriveled up. Others suggest that there's a new ice age coming, and it's only a matter of time until everything becomes so cold that the earth will not be able to support life anymore. Others look at the increasing world population and the decrease in the food available to them; they see the increasing incidence of famine and say that the time is probably coming when the world will no longer be able to support humanity. Others look at the buildup of nuclear weapons and say a holocaust will effectively destroy us and our world.

There are the optimists. There are the pessimists. There are those who feel that people have always survived, that we have tremendous resources of ingenuity, and that we will figure some way out of the predicament in which we find ourselves. There are others who say we are past the point of no return, and it's only a matter of time until the world as we know it will come to an end.

The biblical view of the end of the world

Are you an optimist or a pessimist? I'm neither. I hope I'm a realist. I believe that it is important for us to look into *Scripture* and find out what it says so we're not speculating optimistically or pessimistically. We need to take realistically what the Scriptures tell us about the end. The Bible tells us quite straightforwardly that there is a coming day in which Jesus Christ—who was eternally with the Father, who laid aside his glory, assumed our humanity, lived our life, died our death, and went down into hades and rose again from the dead and ascended to the Father's right hand—one day will return. Into Jesus' hand all judgment has been committed. He will bring things to an end. This fits in with the idea that it is God who initiated, perpetuates, and alone has the authority to terminate our universe. When the God who initiated and continues to perpetuate our world sees fit, he will give the word to his Son, to whom all authority and all judgment has been committed, to bring our world's history to an end.

It's a remarkable thing to consider what the Scriptures teach on this subject. We're relatively comfortable with the baby of Bethlehem, the Incarnation. We're very, very comfortable with that wonderful Jesus who walked the dusty streets of Palestine and laid his hand on the children's heads and said, "Allow the children to come to me." We're highly uncomfortable, but we're deeply moved, by the Christ of the Cross. We understand something of the Resurrection, and we believe something about the Ascension, although when we get into the idea of our own resurrection and ascension, it becomes increasingly vague to us. The idea of Jesus Christ returning in great glory, Jesus Christ coming to terminate all things as we understand them, is quite frightening. It is quite awe-inspiring. To a large extent, many people don't give much thought to it. They hope that the world will just continue on and on as it always has. The Scripture does not give us that freedom. It tells us that the day will come when Christ will return.

The Promise of Christ's Return

Let me talk to you first of all about the revelation that Christ will return. Clearly this is revelation; it is not something we've dreamed up. It is not something that human beings have figured out; it is something that God has revealed to us. And what has he revealed? First of all, he has revealed a basic series of promises. Let me give you some indication of these promises from the words of our Lord Jesus himself. In John 14:1-4 he said,

Do not let your hearts be troubled. Trust in God; trust also in me. In my Father's house are many rooms; if it were not so, I would have told you. I am going there to prepare a place for you. And if I go and prepare a place for you, I will come back and take you to be with me that you also may be where I am. You know the way to the place where I am going.

The discussion had developed around Thomas saying quite bluntly and frankly, "Lord, we don't know where you're going, so how in the world can we know how to get there?"

Jesus responded by saying, "I am the way, the truth, and the life." But sometimes we skip over the beginning of that chapter to get to the juicy verse, "I am the way and the truth and the life. No one comes to the Father except through me." Notice what introduces the discussion: Jesus saying that he was about to depart, and as certainly as he was going to depart, he promised that he would return. The purpose of his return was that his disciples might be with him. Where is he? We've already looked in the creed at the statement that he ascended and sits at the right hand of the Father Almighty. The return that he categorically promised, then, is in order that he might take his disciples into the immediate presence of the living God.

At the Ascension, the disciples were with him, and he was taken from their sight. Acts 1:10 says, "They were looking intently up into the sky as he was going, when suddenly two men dressed in white stood beside them. 'Men of Galilee,' they said, 'why do you stand here looking into the sky?'" I've always felt that was the most unfair question ever asked of a man by an angel! It's obvious why they were standing looking up into the sky: He was there one minute and gone the next. Where in the world did he go? And the angel is asking, "Why are you looking into the sky?" The angels then say these important words: "This same Jesus, who has been taken from you into heaven, will come back in the same way you have seen him go into heaven." So there we have the promise of our Lord Jesus amplified by the angels at the very moment of his ascension. There is a promise in Scripture that Christ will return.

When we look at this promise, we have to examine the possibilities. What does this promise mean? Various theories have been advocated at different times. For instance, some people say Jesus returns for us at death, and the promise of Christ's return simply means that when we die, in a sense, he comes to take us into heaven. There's a problem with this, and while there's an element of truth in it, I believe that if we read Scripture carefully, we'll see that that is not what is intended. For instance, 1 Thessalonians 4:16-17 says,

> The Lord himself will come down from heaven, with a loud command, with the voice of the archangel and with the trumpet call of God, and the dead in Christ will rise first. After that, we who are still alive and are left will be caught up together with them in the clouds to meet the Lord in the air.

Notice that this coming is relevant to those who have already died and to those who are still alive. If his coming simply means he returns for us in death, then why does it say that he is coming for those who are already dead and those who are still alive? Clearly there's a differentiation there. While there's a sense in which Christ comes for us at death, this promise means more than his return when we die.

Other people say that after Jesus had ascended into heaven, he came again in the person of the Holy Spirit at Pentecost. He came as his other self, and the same Spirit of Jesus that indwelt one body was now liberated from the body and was free to come into the body of Christ, that is, all those who are truly believers. So they say that when Christ promised to return, what he was really talking about was the return that he would accomplish in the person of the Holy Spirit on the day of Pentecost.

If we read John 14:15-18, however, I think we'll see that is not what is intended. Jesus said,

"If you love me, you will obey what I command. And I will ask the Father, and he will give you another Counselor to be with you forever—the Spirit of truth. The world cannot accept him, because it neither sees him nor knows him. But you know him, for he lives with you and will be in you. I will not leave you as orphans; I will come to you."

Now notice that there's a degree of ambiguity here, because the Lord Jesus, on the one hand, is saying, "I will ask the Father to send the Spirit," but then, on the other hand, he says, "I will not leave you as orphans; I will come to you." So there is an element of truth in the idea that the return of Christ is accomplished at the day of Pentecost. Clearly there's a sense in which that is true. But there's also the sense in which the Lord Jesus is separating himself from the Holy Spirit, and while he says that in the person of the Holy Spirit there's a sense in which he returns, he is still residing at the Father's right hand. So there's not a full satisfaction of the promise in the return at Pentecost.

Other people say, "Well, what the Scriptures really mean by Jesus' return is that when he comes into our lives at conversion, we're born again of the Spirit of God. That is the return of Christ. This group quotes verses like Revelation 3:20 (KJV), where Jesus said, "Behold, I stand at the door, and knock; if any man hear my voice, and open the door, I will come in to him, and will sup with him, and he with me." However, if we look carefully into what the Scriptures are teaching, it is obvious that there's more to it than Christ returning in conversion.

First Thessalonians 4:14 says, "We believe that Jesus died and rose again and so we believe that God will bring with Jesus those who have fallen asleep in him." Clearly that is not referring to conversion. For when Jesus came into your heart—if you use that expression to explain your conversion—you certainly didn't believe at that time he brought with him all those who have fallen asleep. It's referring to more than this.

There's an element of truth in all these things. He does return at death. He did return at Pentecost. He does come into our lives at conversion. Yet it seems particularly true, from the words of the angels on the day of ascension, that we're talking about a literal return.

When we look at what Paul taught in Thessalonians and in others of the Epistles, he seems to be speaking powerfully in apocalyptic language about a dramatic return of Christ. You remember what the angel said: "This same Jesus, who has been taken from you into heaven, will come back *in the same way*" (Acts 1:11, emphasis mine). This same Jesus in the same way will return. So when we look at what Scripture teaches about the return of Christ, we see the promise, we explore the possibilities, and we come to the conclusion that we're talking about a literal return in glory.

Common Problems with Christ's Return

Having said that, there are problems that we need to address concerning his return. Let me identify three rather common problems. Peter discusses one of the problems in 2 Peter 3:3-4. First of all, he says,

Y ou must understand that in the last days scoffers will come, scoffing and following their own evil desires. They will say, "Where is this 'coming' he promised? Ever since our fathers died, everything goes on as it has since the beginning of creation." But they deliberately forget that long ago by God's word the heavens existed and the earth was formed out of water and by water. By these waters also the world of that time was deluged and destroyed. By the same word the present heavens and earth are reserved for fire, being kept for the day of judgment and destruction of ungodly men.

The problem of unbelief

One of the problems that comes up when we talk about the return of Christ is that some people mock this promise saying, "Come on, the church of Jesus Christ has been talking about this for nineteen hundred years, and he still hasn't come. What makes you think he's coming?" The scoffers that Peter was dealing with in his day went a step further than that. They not only suggested that he hadn't come, but they also said the reason he hadn't come was that he wasn't coming at all. The reason we know that he isn't coming, they would say, is that from the beginning of creation, things have just continued without any sense of dramatic, divine intervention. Peter responds, noting that these critics are carefully forgetting something: There was at least one incident where God dramatically intervened, and that was the Flood. Therefore, those people who operate on the premise that God does not intervene and therefore God has not intervened and will not intervene in the future, are operating on a false premise—because he does intervene. He has intervened and he will intervene and Christ will return.

The problem of date fixing

Some people believe implicitly that Christ will return, and they spend an inordinate amount of time trying to figure out exactly when it will be. This is something that people have done through the centuries. The remarkable thing about it is that they all have one thing in common: they were all wrong. They are not deterred, however! So we still have people who carefully work out exactly when Christ will come again.

As some of you may remember, in 1988 a little booklet came out entitled "88 Reasons Why Christ Will Return in 1988," and it was worked out quite carefully with a vast amount of ingenious reckoning that Christ would come at the feast of Rosh Hashana during a weekend in September. When it was pointed out that the Bible tells us quite clearly that we do not know the day or the hour, then the response simply was, "Well, we may not know the day or the hour, but that doesn't mean we can't know the year and the month and the week," which was rather begging the question.

I remember one of the young women who worked in our church's bookstore came to me one day, and she said, "I'm having a terrible time this week. Our phone is ringing off the hook."

I said, "Why?"

She said, "People are calling and asking, Do we have copies of the booklet '88 Reasons Why Christ Will Return in 1988'? We told them, 'No, we're not stocking it.' And they said, 'Why are you the only Christian bookstore in the city that isn't stocking this book?'" (I don't know if that's true, but that's what they said.) She continued, "I don't know what to say."

So I said, "Tell them to call again at the end of September."

Clearly, Jesus did not return on the date that had been very carefully worked out, and I assumed that the gentlemen who sold a million copies of the booklet would return his royalties, but he didn't, because, you see, people who are busy fixing dates never learn. You know what he then did? He went back to his calculation, found that he had made a slight error, and decided that now Jesus was coming in 1989.

We have a problem here. On the one hand, we have those who frankly disbelieve that he will return, and we have the other people who, even though they've been told that they will not be able to figure out when he is coming, still insist on trying to work it out, and thereby miss the point.

The need for discernment

We have to accept the fact that this area of theology called eschatology is not the easiest. One of the reasons that the interpretation of eschatology is not easy is that much of it is written in dramatic language, which is technically called "apocalyptic literature." The problem with dramatic imagery is that it allows wonderful freedom for all kinds of imagination. And many, many people down through the years have been using all kinds of phenomenal imagination in interpreting the future.

If you check in Revelation 20, there's a statement there about something lasting a thousand years: the millenium. Various theories have developed concerning the millennium. There is a pre-millennial theory: that the Lord Jesus Christ will return and take those who believe in him to be with him, and after his return he will establish a rule on earth for a thousand years. He will come before the millennium; hence this view is termed "pre-millennial." This requires a whole system of biblical interpretation.

Another approach is called post-millennial. This approach assumes that things are going to get better and better until in the end we arrive at a wonderful state of affairs in our world, which will usher in the millennium, and Christ will return at the end of it. Thus, it's called "post-millennial."

Then there are those who say, because what we read in the book of Revelation is figurative, "Why should we take a thousand years as being literal? Why don't we take it as figurative, as we do every other number in the book of Revelation?" This system doesn't support a literal thousand-year reign on earth; hence, the expression "a-millennial." You remember that *a* in the Greek at the beginning of a word means "no" or "negative." There will be no literal millennium.

People who sit in churches, studying escatology, looking into last things have a wonderful time debating all these theories, but there is obviously a problem. We have a lack of discernment. You will find equally committed believers, equally erudite Bible scholars who adopt one of those three positions: pre-, post-, or a-millenial.

Corrie ten Boom was asked one day, "What is your position on the millennium?"

She said, "What do you mean?"

They said, "Are you a-, pre-, or post-?"

"I consider that *a pre-post*erous question," she responded.

Let's be careful before we get into date fixing. Let's be careful if we try to exercise a dogmatism that may be somewhat unwarranted, because these things may take us away from the fundamental, basic thing that we are to understand, that Jesus Christ will return. He will return when he is ready.

You often hear people talking about the imminent return of Christ. That means it could happen any minute. Some people spend their lives on tiptoe in anticipation, expecting Christ to return at any time. My mother was one of those people. My mother lived so practically in the light of the imminent return of Christ that it was absolutely forbidden for us to go to bed until our house and everything that we owned was clean and tidy and perfectly ready to greet him. I think my mother thought he was going to go around and check if the shoes were cleaned and if the pans were all in their places. I can promise you our home was immaculate every night. Now that's a good way to do it, but I'm not quite sure that is why people believe in the imminent return of Christ.

On the one hand, certain biblical passages suggest that many things must take place before Christ returns, and yet, on the other hand, other texts tell us that he could return at any time, even when we least expect him. It can be difficult to pull these two things together. Somebody has suggested that everything in general has been fulfilled for Christ to return, but that he is simply holding off until the appointed time.

Some years ago I conducted a funeral for a helicopter pilot. It was determined that at the conclusion of the burial service there would be a fly pass of helicopters in the traditional missing pilot formation. I was rather intrigued to know how they were going to do this, because they didn't know how long I was going to take for the service. I didn't know, so how could they know how long it was going to take?

Amazingly, at exactly the right moment, just as I concluded the service with the committal words and led the people in prayer and pronounced the amen, there was a *throb-throb-throb-throb* of helicopter engines. Coming low over the trees was the missing comrade formation. Later, I remember turning to the people organizing the funeral and saying, "How in the world did you organize that?" And they said, "Well, actually we knew that you'd finish up with a prayer, and we had somebody with a walkie-talkie. The helicopters were simply circling behind the trees there, slightly over the horizon, and when you were coming to the end of your prayer, we simply talked into the walkie-talkie and called them in."

There's a real sense in which Christ, if we can use the picture, is right on the horizon, waiting for the Father on the walkie-talkie to say, "Go in and get them." In that sense, we have absolutely no idea when he will come. Yet we recognize that he's right on the horizon and when he's ready, he'll come. We have the promise of his return.

Why Will Christ Return?

You may ask, and I hope you do, "What are the reasons that Christ will return?" There are four.

To receive his people

The first reason Christ will return is to receive his own. He will come back in order that those who have committed their lives to him might share his glory and be with him for all eternity. This is how Jesus put it in John 17:24: "Father, I want those you have given me to be with me where I am, and to see my glory, the glory you have given me because you loved me before the creation of the world." That's something that believers look forward to. They look forward to the return of Christ when the Father gives the word, "Go in and get them." He will come in and take those, at the conclusion of earth's history, who belong to him to be with him.

We already noticed in 1 Thessalonians that there are those who have already died in Christ and also those who are still alive at his coming. The order is very simple and basic. As he comes, those who have already died will be raised into his presence in a new way, and those who are still alive will be caught up in the grand reunion around the person of Jesus Christ. Those who are in him will be received by him.

To reward his people

Did you know that there are rewards for those who have honored the Lord and those who have served him faithfully? As Paul writes in 2 Corinthians 5:9-10, "So we make it our goal to please him, whether we are at home in the body or away from it." Here are the important words: "For we must all appear before the judgment seat of Christ, that each one may receive what is due him for the things done while in the body, whether good or bad."

That does not mean that we're going to earn our salvation on the basis of whether we lived a good life or a bad life. We know that the only way we will receive our salvation is through the unmerited favor of God and his grace received by faith. But those who, having received his salvation by grace through faith, have demonstrated their faith in works of service, will be rewarded. Now, I think it's rather futile to try and figure out what these rewards will be. Suffice it to say that they will be commensurate with the grace of our Lord and Savior Jesus Christ and will be appropriate to whatever we have done. He will return to receive his own, and he will return to reward his people.

To reveal his sovereignty

Christ's return will also reveal his sovereignty. As it says in Titus 2:11-13:

> For the grace of God that brings salvation has appeared to all men. It teaches us to say "No" to ungodliness and worldly passions, and to live self-controlled, upright and godly lives in this present age, while we wait for the blessed hope—the glorious appearing of our great God and Savior, Jesus Christ.

Notice how Jesus is described here, "our great God and Savior." Don't you get the feeling of majesty? Don't you get the feeling of sovereignty? Don't you get the tremendous feeling of him being numero uno, in charge, generalissimo, with the name above every name and the title above every title? He is coming to demonstrate—on a cosmic scale—his total, absolute, irrevocable, undeniable lordship. He will be seen by every eye. Every knee will bow to him, and every tongue will confess that he truly is Lord, to the glory of God the Father. So when Christ returns he will come to receive his own. He will come to reward his people. He will come to reveal his sovereignty.

To rebuke his foes

Finally, Christ will come to rebuke his foes. Remember how the creed puts it: "Hence he shall come *to judge the quick and the dead*" (emphasis mine). We're not now thinking of the babe of Bethlehem. Neither are we thinking of the gentle Savior, meek and mild. Neither are we thinking of the suffering servant on the cross. We're thinking now of the great judge before whom heaven and earth will flee. There is not one person who will not stand before the one, Jesus Christ, into whose hands God has committed all judgment.

When the great judgment comes, Christ will determine who are the sheep and who are the goats. The quick and the dead will be there. The small and the great will be there, and it will make no difference. Jesus Christ is the one who will judge all people, and the determining factor is going to be what our attitude was toward Christ as Savior and Lord. That's why he's coming: to rebuke his foes, to reveal his sovereignty, to reward his people, and to receive his own.

Implications of Christ's Return for the Ungodly

We recognize that Christ will return. What does this mean for the ungodly? What does it mean for the godly? I want to leave you with three very simple statements.

Utopianism is misplaced optimism

Goethe, the German philosopher, says, "Humanity marches ever forward, but man always stays the same." There is a utopianism abroad in some areas where people—humanists, technologically oriented people—are absolutely convinced that humans and technology and science can solve all our problems and will eventually produce utopia, that glorious place where everything is absolutely perfect. But Goethe points out with rare insight that humanity is always moving on, yet man always stays the same.

Or, put another way, we know how to put man on the moon, but we haven't the remotest idea how to get man to live on earth. Our technology is brilliant. What we can solve with our ingenuity is mind-blowing. But we can't fix man. He's still as ornery; he's still as sinful; he's still as destructive; he's still as rebellious as he ever was. There is no improvement whatsoever. Utopianism is a misplaced optimism. Our world is not going to finish up in a utopian paradise. Our world is going to finish up before the judgment of Christ. He will terminate it.

Universalism is a misguided dream

Some people say, "Everything is going to work out all right in the end, and God is a loving god, and therefore he's going to gather everybody into heaven," but the apostle Paul tells us that the judgment that God has committed into the hands of Jesus Christ is going to be based on reality. There may be many ways of hoodwinking the legal system. There may be many ways in which the legal system itself is inadequate or even erroneous. But the judgment that God will execute through his Son is based on total reality and utter truth. That means that there is good and evil, right and wrong, and the great judge will separate between sheep and goats, good and evil, right and wrong. Universalism is a misguided dream.

Utilitarianism is a mistaken philosophy

Utilitarianism is the approach to life that says basically, "If it feels good, if it looks good, if it does good, it must be all right." That is basically how many people in our society operate today. But we need to notice something. When God judges you and me, it will not be on the basis of whether it felt good to us. When he judges you and me, it will be on the basis of righteousness, whether we did that which was right before him. He won't ask us, Did it look good? He won't ask us, Did you feel good? He'll ask us, Were you good? And did you do good? Looking good and feeling good are the basic interests in our society today. In heaven the interests are not looking good and feeling good. In heaven the interests are being good and doing good. That is the basis of the judgment. Therefore, utilitarianism is a mistaken philosophy.

We need to make sure that if we believe firmly in the return of Christ, we believe that he will come whenever God speaks into his walkie-talkie and says, "Go in and get them," and terminates this earth's history. If we believe that, we need to have a concern for those utopianists, those universalists, those utilitarian people who are simply building their lives on sinking sand.

Implications of Christ's Return for the Godly

But what about the godly people? What does the recognition of Christ's return do for them? I suggest four things.

Be ready

In Matthew 25, the story of an Eastern wedding ceremony, the bridegroom would come from his home and start walking down toward the place of the marriage, and the bridesmaids would be ready with their lamps. On this particular occasion the bridegroom was delayed, so they grew careless and some of them weren't prepared when he came. They never got into the feast. This story is unmistakably clear: The godly must live in a state of readiness.

Be supportive

When Paul was writing to the Thessalonians, he was explaining to the Thessalonian Christians, who were relatively new believers, what had happened to those who had already died, and he said, "Listen; let me explain to you. Those who have already died are going to be with Christ when he returns, and those who are still alive will be with Christ when he returns. Therefore, encourage each other with these words." The believers who believe in the return of Christ live in a state of readiness and constantly exhibit an attitude of supportiveness.

Be holy

We are constantly encouraging those who are bereaved. We're constantly teaching those who are unsure. We're telling them about our great and glorious hope. Peter, in the passage about the mockers, goes on to explain that when the Lord returns, the heavens and earth will dissolve with fervent heat, and a new heaven and a new earth will be built, characterized by righteousness. Then he asks a rhetorical question. He says, Seeing these things are going to be dissolved, what sort of people ought we to be? Since it is a rhetorical question, he answers it himself: We should be characterized by a commitment to holiness.

Be purposeful

Matthew 24:14 is the final word on what the return of Christ means to the godly. It says this: "This gospel of the kingdom will be preached in the whole world as a testimony to all nations, and then will come the end." This means that those who genuinely believe in the return of Christ should have a tremendous sense of purposefulness about them because they realize that when Christ comes, the day of grace will be over. They realize that at this moment of time there are many millions of people who need to know about Christ, and their lives have a sense of urgency and purposefulness about them.

The doctrine of Christ's return, to judge the quick and the dead, is a powerful doctrine indeed. For it reminds those who are careless about spiritual things that the day of opportunity might slip away from them, and it reminds those who are committed to Jesus Christ that they are called to purposefulness, readiness, and holiness. That's why he has told us these things.

Now let me ask you a couple of questions. Are you ready for Jesus Christ to return? Have you made your peace with God? Have you committed your life to Jesus as your Savior and Lord so that when he returns for you, either personally, with death, or in great glory to consummate his eternal purposes and to end this world's history, you will be ready? Either way, when he returns, will you be found among those who are his?

Let me ask you another question. Do you profess to be a believer? Are you living in the light of his return? And is your life characterized by readiness, holiness, and purposefulness? You see, it is when we consider these things in the light of his return that we have tremendous incentive to get our lives right before the Lord.

MAKING IT PRACTICAL

1. What are four reasons Scripture gives for Christ's return?

2. Describe three theories that try to explain Christ's return. What are the problems with these explanations?

3. What is the world's response to the thought that someday it will all come to an end? What should the church's response be in regard to the end of the world?

4. What are three implications of the return of Christ for those who do not believe?

5. How does your thinking about Christ's return affect the way you live? How ought we to live in light of this fact?

10

"The Holy Spirit"

John 16:5-15

The first part of the Apostle's Creed has to do with God the Father and his work of creation. The second segment has to do with God the Son and his work of redemption. The third and final part of the creed has to do with God the Holy Spirit and his work of transformation. Here we consider what it means to believe in God the Holy Spirit.

In John 16:5 we read some of the final words of our Lord Jesus to his disciples:

> Now I am going to him who sent me, yet none of you asks me, "Where are you going?" Because I have said these things, you are filled with grief. But I tell you the truth: It is for your good that I am going away. Unless I go away, the Counselor will not come to you; but if I go, I will send him to you. When he comes, he will convict the world of guilt in regard to sin and righteousness and judgment: in regard to sin, because men do not believe in me; in regard to righteousness, because I am going to the Father, where you can see me no longer; and in regard to judgment, because the prince of this world now stands condemned.
>
> "I have much more to say to you, more than you can now bear. But when he, the Spirit of truth, comes, he will guide you into all truth. He will not speak on his own; he will speak

145

only what he hears, and he will tell you what is yet to come. He will bring glory to me by taking from what is mine and making it known to you. All that belongs to the Father is mine. That is why I said the Spirit will take from what is mine and make it known to you." *John 16:5-15*

It is imperative that we understand what it means to believe in the Holy Spirit because there is a considerable degree of confusion. There are those, of course, who do not believe in God in three persons: God the Father, God the Son, and God the Holy Spirit.

In the same way that they would relegate the Son to an inferior position, so, of course, they would relegate the Holy Spirit to an inferior position. Scripture, however, speaks forcibly about the fact of the Holy Spirit and his identity.

The deity of the Holy Spirit

In John 16 there's an intertwining of the activities and the relationships of the Father, the Son, and the Holy Spirit. In verse 15 John says, "All that belongs to the Father is mine. That is why I said the Spirit will take from what is mine and make it known to you." There is an interrelationship between the Father, the Son, and the Spirit. You will remember that in the great commission recorded for us in Matthew 28:19, the disciples were told to go into all the world and make disciples, baptizing them in the name of the Father and of the Son and of the Holy Spirit. There's a grammatical curiosity there, for it says the *name* (singular) of Father, Son, and Holy Spirit, reminding us that there is one God manifest in three persons.

In the benediction that comes at the end of Paul's Corinthian letters, Paul prays that the love of God, the grace of our Lord Jesus, and the fellowship of the Holy Spirit might be experienced by all. And there are many, many other ways in which in Scripture we have the clear sense of the deity of the Holy Spirit.

The personality of the Holy Spirit

Unfortunately, in some of the older Bibles, the Holy Spirit is sometimes talked about as an "it," in sort of a neuter sense. But you'll notice, in the passage I pointed out, the Lord Jesus speaks of him as a "he," suggesting personality. There are many qualities of a person that are attributed to the Holy Spirit. It is possible to have a relationship with the Holy Spirit. For instance, Paul told the Ephesian Christians, "Grieve not the Holy Spirit." You can only grieve a person; you can't grieve an idea, a force, or an impersonal entity. So the Holy Spirit is seen as deity, and he's also seen as personality.

The energy of the Holy Spirit

But there's also a clear sense in which there's a connotation of energy when we talk about the Holy Spirit. The Greek word translated "spirit" is *pneuma,* from which we get *pneumatic.* The Hebrew word for spirit is *ruach.* And these two have one thing in common: Their original meaning is "breeze" or "wind." Sometimes the symbols of the Holy Spirit speak of him as a breeze or a wind, an energetic force.

Some of us, from our early days, will remember being confused about the fact that there was God the Father, God the Son, and a Holy "Ghost." This was kind of weird. That's because our understanding of the term *ghost* has changed dramatically. The original idea of a ghost was that it was the spiritual energy resident within a person, and when a person died, that spiritual energy was released. So, in that sense, it's perfectly valid to speak of the Holy Spirit as the Holy Ghost—the wind, the breeze, the energy of God.

It's a good rule of thumb that whenever God does anything big, the Holy Spirit is clearly in evidence. When God was active in creation, the Spirit of God "was hovering over the waters;" he was an energetic force in creation. When God sent his Son into the world in the Incarnation, he was conceived by the Holy Spirit. When the Lord Jesus went into the wilderness to confront, head to head, the evil one, we read that he was led there by the Spirit, and after the great conflict, he came out in the power of the Spirit. When the Lord Jesus went to the cross for our redemption, Hebrews tells us it was through the eternal Spirit that he offered himself. When God wants to raise him from the dead, Paul reminds us of "the Spirit of him that raised up Christ from the dead." And so in creation, in incarnation, in temptation, in crucifixion, in resurrection, the Holy Spirit is indeed the energy of God.

Then what happened? We got the Scriptures—the Scriptures that are food for our souls, the Scriptures that are our life itself. It's no surprise to discover that Peter tells us the Scriptures were written when holy men of old were carried along by the Holy Spirit. When Paul reminds Timothy that all Scripture is God-breathed, the same idea comes out—Spirit-breathed, Spirit motivated—and that is why they are inspired for our good. When God does anything big in a person's life in regeneration, it is because that person has been born of the Spirit. So the rule of thumb applies that whenever God is energetically moving in the affairs of men, his Spirit is the energy of this activity. In creation, incarnation, temptation, crucifixion, resurrection, inspiration, and regeneration, the Spirit is at work.

The activity of the Spirit is what the Lord Jesus speaks about in John 16. Notice two particular directions of his activity: first of all, toward the believer; secondly, toward the unbelieving world.

The Activity of the Spirit toward Believers

Notice that in verse 7 the Lord Jesus says, "Unless I go away, the Counselor will not come to you; but if I go, I will send him to you." Those of you who are familiar with older versions of the Bible will find the world *Counselor* a little unusual. You are used to the word *Comforter.* The Greek word translated either "comforter" or "counselor" is *parakletos.* That is a composite Greek word from *para,* which means alongside, like parachurch, which is alongside the church, or a paramedic, who works alongside the medical community, and *kaleo* means "to call." So *parakletos* is someone who is called alongside.

Parakletos. That is the title given to the Holy Spirit. The one called alongside may be there to comfort, or in a legal sense, to act as a defense attorney. However, the preponderance of evidence suggests that the idea of counselor is what is intended, that the Holy Spirit is one called alongside to speak on our behalf and also on behalf of the one who has sent him.

But the idea of comforter is appropriate too, particularly when we bear in mind the etymology of the word *comfort.* When we talk about comfort, we usually mean we're making somebody comfortable, helping them feel good, helping them relax. But the etymology of the word *comfort* comes from the Latin *con fortes,* which means "to strengthen with." Literally and basically, the idea of comforting is to come alongside someone to give them strength and encouragement, to make them strong, and to speak on their behalf. That is the concept of the Holy Spirit, the *parakletos.* And this is what he has in mind for us when the Holy Spirit comes into our lives.

Notice in John 14:16 that the Lord Jesus talks of him as another parakletos. The word *another* is important there. There are different Greek words for *another.* This one means "another of the same kind." That means there's another parakletos somewhere. If you check in 1 John 2:1, you'll find that the Lord Jesus is called the parakletos. He is one who is called alongside the Father—Jesus Christ the righteous one. He speaks to the Father on our behalf. We talked about this when we dealt with the passage that said Jesus ascended to the Father's right hand. He is there in the immediate presence of God as our representative. In the same way, the parakletos, the Holy Spirit, is present in our lives as the divine representative to strengthen, to encourage, to console, and to speak on God's behalf.

The Spirit is truth

Notice also, in John 14:17, that the Counselor is also called the Spirit of truth. The Spirit of truth. That's a very important title for the Holy Spirit. He deals in what is true and real, as opposed to what is deceitful and counterfeit. This needs to be stressed in our present age.

Not so many years ago, we worshipped technology and looked to science to solve all our problems. But we've soured a bit on science and technology because now some of us are thinking, maybe instead of solving our problems, science and technology are contributing to our problems. So people have tended to move away from a technological, scientific approach to a tremendous interest in the spirit world. There's great interest in esoteric things. This is both good and bad. If this interest in the spirit world is opening us up to the possibility that God by his Spirit is working in our lives and that God by his Spirit is the answer to our problems, rather than technology, that's good. But if our openness to the spirit is an openness to a spirit world that is not a spirit of truth, then the possibilities of deception are immense.

Recently a young high school student committed suicide. His girlfriend and his family were understandably distraught about this terrible event. The girlfriend, however, was contacted by some other girls in the school who were dabbling, just for the fun of it, they thought, with seances and Ouija boards. They said they could get in touch with her boyfriend's spirit. So she went along, and in this particular experience, they got in touch with the spirits. The spirits spoke to them and told these young girls to tell the girlfriend that her boyfriend wanted her to join him, and that she should commit suicide because then she could really enjoy his presence. That is not the spirit of truth; that's the spirit of evil. That is the spirit of utter deceit, and it's abroad in our world today.

Many people in our society are becoming increasingly intrigued with things of the spirit that are not the Spirit of truth. We can evaluate what the spirit is saying by finding out if it contradicts the

Bible. If it contradicts the Bible, it is not of the Holy Spirit. And so we recognize his work in our lives as the Spirit of truth.

The Spirit brings holiness

Notice also in verse 26 of John 14 that he is called the Holy Spirit. If the Spirit of truth is interested in truthfulness, the Holy Spirit is concerned about holiness. Often the interest in things spiritual is leading people into activities that are far removed from holy living. When we see that that is the case, we know it is not the Holy Spirit they are contacting. They are dealing with seducing spirits. We can always be sure that the Spirit of God is at work in our lives when he points us to the Father and to the Son, when he leads us into the truth, and produces holiness in our lives.

The Spirit is working

In John 15:26 we see that the Counselor is going to come because the Lord Jesus would send him from the Father. He's the Spirit of truth who goes out from the Father.

Notice all the sending that's going on here. The Father is sending the Son, and the Son returns and asks the Father to send the Holy Spirit. Notice the pictures of interrelatedness. The Son, having been sent and completed his ministry, is subsequently followed by the Holy Spirit to do his ministry.

When I was a teenager (hundreds of years ago!), I remember going to a meeting in Manchester, England, that we called a "squash." The reason we called those meetings a squash was that they were held for young people in private homes, and we squashed as many people into a room as we possibly could. All the furniture was taken out; the teenagers were just squashed in on the floor. The speaker was given the only chair in the room. On this particular occasion, the speaker was Montague Goodman. He sat there, wagged his finger at us, and said, "Young people, I am an octogenarian." I thought that that was some kind of a vegetarian, but someone told me, "No, he means he's over eighty." And I said, "Well, why doesn't he just say that?" But he worked on the principle that he never used a short word if a long one would do. (You know what Churchill said about that, don't you? "Anybody who uses a long word when a short one will do, I find that practice utterly reprehensible.")

He went on to say that when God completed his work on the seventh day, he sat down. And he sent his Son into the world, who, when he completed his work of redemption, ascended to the Father's right hand and sat down. "Now, young people," he said, "I want you to check in your Bibles and find out where the Holy Spirit, whom the Son sent into the world, has sat down. Where does it say that?" He said, "Well, I'll help you. It doesn't say that. The reason, young people, is simply this, that the Father's work of creation was completed, and he figuratively sat down. The Son's work of redemption was completed, and he figuratively sat down. And the work of the Holy Spirit is not completed. He is the member of the Trinity with whom we primarily have to deal."

So, here's the picture. The Holy Spirit comes, another parakletos, the Spirit of truth, sent by the Father, and the Lord Jesus adds, It is better for you if I go away. The disciples don't agree with that. They're grieving this imminent departure, but he explains to them, Listen, when I'm gone, you'll do greater things than I ever did.

No, they say, we couldn't do that. But they did.

The first time Peter got up and preached, three thousand people were converted. We don't know of three thousand people converted in thirty-three years when Jesus preached. Remarkable things are happening because the Spirit of God is alive in people's lives. But that wasn't all he meant when he said it's better for you if I go. What he meant was that while he was living in a human body, he was localized. But when he ascended to the Father, he would send his Holy Spirit into the lives of innumerable believers, and the same Spirit who had energized the Son would now move into our lives. The parakletos would come to dwell within us. That's what we mean when we say, "I believe in the Holy Spirit." He's not only the parakletos, however; he is also the teacher.

The Spirit is a teacher

In John 14:26 the Lord Jesus says that when the comforter comes he "will teach you all things and will remind you of everything I have said to you." And in 16:13 he also tells us that he will guide us into all truth. Notice those three words that have to do with the teaching activity of the Holy Spirit: *teaching, reminding,* and *guiding.* How does the Holy Spirit teach us? The Holy Spirit inspired the Word of God, and we read the Word of God on a regular basis. We learn of the Holy Spirit when we recognize that God's Word is as important as food. You can't live by bread alone, yet you take some of that every day. You're going to need to be taught by the Spirit through the Word every day as well.

In addition, the Holy Spirit gives and anoints certain people for a preaching and teaching ministry. Notice what's important there: It's not the person. It is the Holy Spirit who calls; it is the Holy Spirit who anoints. When that gifted, anointed, called person takes the inspired Word and proclaims it to people under the power of the Holy Spirit, what happens? The Holy Spirit begins to teach people. That does not mean that the preacher is infallible, however. And the safeguard against this is that the believer has the witness of the Spirit within. When the preacher takes the Word, and under the empowering of the Holy Spirit speaks the truth, your spirit and the Holy Spirit agree, and there's an inner sense of what J. B. Phillips called "the ring of truth." That is why we spend time in the Word daily; we make it a top priority, along with worship and attending to the preaching and teaching of the Word of God.

We also move in the community of God's people. We build relationships where people indwelt by the Holy Spirit can interface with our lives, creating a place where there's a networking of spirits, of lives, and of concerns. Through the Word, through preaching and teaching, and through the fellowship with the community of saints, God's Spirit teaches us.

The Spirit is our reminder

He doesn't just teach us; he reminds us. I've heard people say, "That's great! The Holy Spirit is just going to remind me, so I don't need to study or listen to teachers. When I need something, the Holy Spirit will bring it to my remembrance." If you're thinking like that, let me tell you one thing: You cannot be reminded of something you never knew. So when it says the Holy Spirit will bring something to your remembrance, it doesn't mean that is a substitute for study. What it means is that the product of your study will be brought to your recollection at the right time by the Holy Spirit to achieve his purposes.

I was invited to go to Jackson, Mississippi, to speak to a crowd of theological students and pastors. I had a great time down there. While I was flying there I was thinking in the back of my mind, *I have to talk to the staff on Monday morning, and I need to get something ready to say to them.* As I was thinking that, sitting in the airplane, it was as if a voice inside my head rang through with a verse, a statement that I didn't know I knew. But I knew that I had to talk to the staff about it. I didn't know where it came from, so when I got to Jackson, I went into the library, got a concordance, and looked. Sure enough, I found it there. It was a verse from Scripture that I didn't even remember I knew. But somewhere along the line, I'd taken the trouble to learn it, and God had something to say to the staff through me that morning. I'm certain of this because years ago the Spirit taught it to me, and then the Holy Spirit brought it to my remembrance in order that I might minister what the Spirit wanted to say to the staff. That's what the Holy Spirit does.

The Spirit guides us into truth

The Lord Jesus wants us to know his will and his purpose. And he's not hiding them from us. The Holy Spirit comes into our lives and ministers through the Word and through our brothers and sisters and gives us that inner sense of witness of our spirit with the Holy Spirit as to what he wants us to do. This doesn't mean that he whispers, "Wear a yellow tie." I don't think he cares what color tie you wear. (Between you and me, I don't think he cares if you wear a tie. I doubt that Jesus ever wore a tie in his life. It would look weird with the kind of clothes he did wear. But I like ties; they are good for hanging microphones on, but they serve no other useful purpose.) The Holy Spirit isn't going to bother telling you things like that. But when you have a desire to know what he wants you to do, I believe through the very structures in the fellowship of believers the Holy Spirit will give you a sense of what is the way to go. He is our teacher.

The Spirit is our enabler

In addition, the Holy Spirit is our enabler. Notice that the Lord Jesus, in John 14:15, says, "If you love me, you will obey what I command." And you say, "Oh boy, this obedience thing is the biggest stumbling block for me. I know what I should do, but I don't always do it. I don't even want to do it sometimes. And so I get a bit worried when he says, 'If you love me, you'll obey what I command.' I think I love him, but I'm not always obedient. I don't always want to be obedient. What's wrong?" Well, I'll tell you what's wrong.

The Holy Spirit, when he comes into our lives, begins to change our desires, our aspirations, our wants, and our longings. One of the things he changes is the desire to obey rather than the desire to disobey, and a craving to be dependent on God, rather than the world's sense of wanting to be independent. Not only that, as he begins to change our orientation, he gives us the power to obey. God didn't lean out of heaven and say, "Do this and do that; don't do this and don't do that; and if you don't, I'll zap you." Instead he said, "If you love me, you'll obey me, and you'll be able to obey me because I will enable you by the Holy Spirit."

The thing to remember is this: If God ever told you to do anything, at the same time he told you to do it, he empowered you by his Spirit. So you can never say to one of God's commands, "I can't!" because that would deny the enabling power of the Holy Spirit. All you can say is, "I won't." And that would remind you of your disobedience. So there's an enabling by the Holy Spirit that makes us willing to obey.

Notice also that he says to ask the Father and he will grant us things in prayer. Another thing that the Holy Spirit enables us to do is learn how to pray. So often we don't know what to pray. We don't know if we should pray it, but we've already seen that the Holy Spirit works in our heart, gives us an understanding of God's mind and purpose, and gives us desires that equate his desires. In his name we can pray with assurance, and as we do that, he begins to move in and answer our prayers. In John 15:26, talking about the Spirit when he comes, he says, "He will testify about me." He also adds immediately, "And you also must testify" (verse 27). It is ridiculous to think that I can testify effectively to Christ and have anything happen. You say, "Oh, the Holy Spirit can do that." That's ridiculous, too. You see, the balance is this: When the Holy Spirit comes, he will testify about Christ, but that doesn't mean that we don't have to do it too.

In other words, we will know what to say because the Holy Spirit will give us the words to speak. The Lord Jesus said quite categorically to his disciples on one occasion, "When I'm gone they'll give you a hard time, and they'll haul you in front of the authorities, and they'll really stick it to you." Then he added, "But don't worry about what you're going to say. It will be given to you in that same hour what you shall speak." That's what the Holy Spirit does. He makes us willing to obey, he teaches us how to pray, and he helps us know what to say. This is his enabling ministry.

The Spirit as the indweller

The Spirit is also the indweller. In John 14:17, this is what the Lord Jesus says when he speaks of the comforter, the counselor: "He lives with you and will be in you." As a result of that he says, "I will come to you" (verse 18). And as a result of that he says, "Because I live, you also will live." That's referring to the indwelling presence of God the Holy Spirit. Get the picture of the Trinity? God the Father has concluded his work of creation and is seated on his throne. God the Son completed his work of redemption and is seated at the Father's right hand. The Holy Spirit is active in the world today, in the hearts and lives of believers, energetically doing God's work of transformation in believers' lives and in the community of the church. That's what we mean when we talk about believing in the Holy Spirit.

The Activity of the Spirit and Unbelievers

In verse 8 of chapter 16, John says, when the counselor comes, "he will convict the world of guilt in regard to sin and righteousness and judgment." Notice that the activity of the Holy Spirit toward the unbelieving world is that of convicting. The Greek word here is *elencho*. It's an important word to remember. Remember what we said about *parakletos* being like the defense attorney? The word *elencho* is the word used to describe the activity of a prosecuting attorney: bringing conviction, challenging people, prosecuting people. So here we see the other side of the ministry of the

Holy Spirit. To the believer he is the defense attorney. To the unbeliever he is the prosecuting attorney. He brings a tremendous sense of guilt to the unbelieving world.

The Spirit convicts of sin

Psychologists have been very helpful in identifying different kinds of guilt. There is the kind of guilt that some people suffer from because of abusive families they were raised in. There's the kind of guilt that some people suffer from because of unrealistic demands they place upon themselves. When you've got a situation like that, you need counseling to help you get out from under this unrealistic guilt.

The problem, however, is this. Sometimes psychologists try to get rid of the guilt that belongs there because the Holy Spirit is convicting us of sin. That is why we need skilled counselors who not only understand psychology, but are deeply taught in theology too, so that they can differentiate between real guilt and false guilt. What a terrible thing it is to tell somebody who is suffering because of parental abuse that this is the Holy Spirit who is convicting them of sin.

But what a dreadful thing it is to tell someone who is convicted by the Holy Spirit that their guilt is a false guilt! How wrong it is to imply that someone shouldn't feel guilty about the unrighteousness the Holy Spirit is leading them to repent of. We must be sensitive to the fact that the Holy Spirit convicts people and prosecutes people about sin and righteousness and the judgment to come.

The Lord Jesus amplified this when he said it will be necessary for the Holy Spirit to convict people of sin, and the reason will be "because men do not believe in me." What he is saying is that while we talk about sin in various categories, the essence of sin is unbelief. The essence of sin is independence. Sin is refusal to acknowledge God as God, enthroned in my life. When I enthrone myself, I am perfectly capable of refusing to heed the call of the Holy Spirit in my life.

So who is enthroned in your life? You, or the holy trinity of God, Jesus, and the Holy Spirit? The choice you make will affect not only your eternal destiny, but the lives of those around you, in the world today and the world to come.

MAKING IT PRACTICAL

1. What are some of the many things the Holy Spirit does for the believer?

2. How does the Holy Spirit affect the unbeliever?

3. Describe evidence you see every day of a profound interest in the spirit world. What are the dangers of this interest?

4. What is your perception of the Holy Spirit? How does this affect how he works in and what he does through you?

11

"The Holy Catholic Church"

Matthew 16:13-20

Some people regard the church as an article of belief. Others, sadly, find it to be an obstacle to belief. It's not uncommon to find people who are open to spiritual life but not to life in the church. It's not uncommon to find people who have a certain degree of commitment to Jesus but are not at all interested in any commitment to a visible representation of his church. And then, of course, there are people who feel that the worst thing that ever happened to Christ was that he was saddled with the church.

In England some years ago, there was a very colorful, outspoken politician called Lord Beothby, who wrote a book entitled, *What I Believe.* This is one of the things he said:

The history of the Christian churches has been one of atrocious cruelty. All of them have done untold harm to the world. The traditions of the Christian churches for centuries can be summarized as dogma, persecution, secession, hatred, destruction, and fire. In fact, everything that Jesus loathed and denounced.

Notice the point at the end there, that he is not opposing Jesus. He's not opposing what Jesus taught. But he feels that the church of

Jesus Christ has had a centuries-long tradition of counteracting all that Jesus taught. And that it actually has propagated all that he loathed and denounced. Although that's a scathing denunciation of the church, those of us who are committed to the church have to admit that our history is by no means all that it might have been.

There are many people who have soured on the church. I have to admit that that was exactly my situation at one stage in my spiritual experience. Jill and I were deeply concerned about the youth of Britain at the time. There were thousands upon thousands of them who never darkened the door of a church. And the people who sat in the church were highly critical of the kids. One day I asked some of these critical people in the church, "Have you ever sat down and talked to these kids?" I discovered that most of them had not. I hadn't either, so I decided that perhaps I should. To cut a long story short, we began to reach out to these young people who were spending their time in the coffeehouses of Britain at that time. It was the era of the Beatles, so you can imagine I'm talking about a time just shortly after the Middle Ages.

As I got to know these young people, I discovered all kinds of fascinating things about them. I discovered that they were deeply interested in spiritual matters, that they were totally open to Jesus Christ, and they had a deep antipathy toward the church. I discovered something else. If I tried to work with these kids and gradually introduce them into the churches, the antipathy of the churches toward these kids was equalled only by the antipathy of these kids to the church. There was a total standoff.

I remember watching a Billy Graham movie in which a character played by Cliff Richards confronts an English vicar and says to him, "If I were Jesus Christ and came back and saw what you'd done to my church, I'd sue you." The whole place erupted in applause, and I joined in. I was deeply committed to Jesus Christ. I was spending all my spare time preaching, evangelizing, and reaching young people, but as far as the church was concerned, I had not had good experiences with it. I didn't feel it was doing its job. I felt, quite frankly, we were doing what the church should have been doing all along, and all we got was criticism from church people as we were doing it.

What happened to me then? I'm glad you asked. One day a friend of mine said to me, "Stuart, I have a problem with you."

And I said, "What is it?"

He replied, "You insist that you're all in favor of Jesus Christ, but you're not in favor of what Jesus was all in favor of."

I said, "What do you mean?"

"Jesus Christ," he said, "loved the church. He gave himself for the church. He washed the church in his own blood, and he longs for the day when the church might be gathered to him in eternity. He is absolutely, totally committed to the church. He said, 'It's my church and I'm going to build it, and the gates of Hades will not overcome it.' How in the world can you say you're all in favor of Christ and his cause when you are so negative and critical of that which he loves and gave himself for?"

He did me a world of good, that good friend of mine. He gave me a good talking to, and I realized that I had to decide whether I believed what Jesus said about the church or whether I was simply going to go on with my own critical attitudes toward it. Well, you know the end of the story. The end of the story is that I deeply wanted to become a pastor of a church, so that I could not only commit myself to Jesus Christ, but commit myself to the ministry and life of a fellowship of believers. So I believe in the church, but I understand people who have a hard time with it.

Of course, the rest of the article is that we believe in the *holy* church. When some people say that line in the creed, they have a hard time not giggling. Other people cross their fingers when they say it. They think, *Well, I don't really mean this, but it's there, so I guess I'd better say it.* But I believe, not only in the church, but I believe in the truer sense of the word, that the church is holy. Then we have the expression "I believe in the holy *catholic* church." As soon as you mention the word *catholic* you'll find that to some people it's like a red rag to a bull: They'll really go for it. On the other hand, many people find this word deeply significant.

I want to tell you three things: Number one, I believe in the church. Number two, I believe the church is holy. Number three, I believe the church is catholic. And I'll spend the rest of this chapter explaining what I mean.

I Believe in the Church

What do we mean when we profess in the creed, "I believe in the church"? The meaning of the word *church* is significant. The English or the American word *church* comes from the Old English, which was pronounced more or less the same way but spelled quite differently. That word was related to the Scottish word for church, which is *kirk,* and the German word, which is *kirche.*

I have problems pronouncing German words with an English tongue. For instance, the word for "cherry" and the word for "church" are very similar in German. And that's why one time when I was preaching in German, I couldn't understand why everybody was laughing, and it was because I preached a moving sermon entitled; "On this rock I will build my cherry!"

All these words have their root in a Greek word, *kuriake* or *kuriakon,* meaning simply "what belongs to the Lord." *Kurios* is "Lord." *Kuriake* means "belonging to the Lord." The etymology of this English word *church* is simply a word that means "belonging to the Lord." That gives us the first clue when we're talking about church. The Greek word that is translated "church" in the New Testament is *ekklesia. Ekklesia* comes from two Greek words that mean literally "to call out from." And so the second idea of the church is that the church is something that belongs to the Lord, that is "called out from."

It isn't just called out from, but it is called out from to be gathered to. And so the idea of church is that it is something that belongs to the Lord that he has called out from the world to be gathered to himself. You'll find in the Old Testament a Hebrew word *qahal,* which related to the people of God in the wilderness.

In the Greek New Testament, they're called the *ekklesia*. We put all this together and get a definition of church. Church is something that belongs uniquely to the Lord, comprised entirely of people God has called out from the world to be gathered to himself.

Often when we talk about church, we've got either a building or an institution in mind, but in actual fact, the real meaning of church is people who belong to Christ and unitedly are committed to his cause. Church is not somewhere you go; church is something you are. We are the church of God that happens to meet in a particular facility.

What then is the purpose of this church? Surely God could have accomplished all that he needed to do simply by calling out individuals and letting them go their individual ways. But he decided not to do that; he decided that the church was significant. Ephesians 1:22-23 contains three clues about the significance of the church or the purpose of the church. Speaking of Christ, it says this: "And God placed all things under his feet and appointed him to be head over everything for the church, which is his body, the fullness of him who fills everything in every way."

The first answer to our question "What is the purpose of the church?" is simply this: to be the body of Christ. What does that mean? Let me illustrate for you. The particular facility in which Elmbrook is meeting at this present time did not exist at one time. It was decided that we should move out to a particular site and build a facility in which the church could meet. The architect invited anybody in our congregation at that time to come and talk to him about what they felt should be incorporated. People stood in line to tell him. He took notes. We got it all together. We calculated and found it would cost 1.75 billion dollars to incorporate everything that everybody wanted. So we decided to change. But he did ask me if I had any preferences. I said, yes, I had two or three.

"What are they?"

I said, "I'd like the pulpit to be central in the geometric center of the building" (which, incidentally, it is.) "Secondly, I'd like it to be circular."

He said, "Why?"

I said, "Because when the Lord taught people, they gathered around him, and I think it's the best use of space. Also, it gives the feeling of fellowship. You can't have fellowship with the back of people's heads."

The third thing I pointed out to him was that I would like a gallery for the spirits. He'd been taking notes, and suddenly he looked up. He said, "A what?"

"A gallery for the spirits."

"What are you talking about?" he asked.

"It seems to me that all the expense of building a facility for a church is related to the bodies of people, so many inches per derriere. That's what architects work on. You didn't realize that, did you? So many square feet in the foyer, heating for bodies, cooling for bodies, lighting for bodies, room to park cars in which bodies come. All the expense is for bodies," I told him.

He said, "You're right."

I said, "I know how we can save a lot of money."

He said, "How?"

"By having a gallery for spirits. It will be very small. We don't need to heat it, don't need to cool it, don't need to light it; the spirits will be perfectly happy there."

"What spirits are you talking about?" he asked.

I said, "The spirits of all those people who week after week tell me, 'Sorry we can't be with you this summer, Stuart, but we'll be with you in spirit.' "

And he said, "British humor, I suppose."

And I said, "Yes."

But he said, "You have a point, because if you ain't there in your body, you ain't there."

And that's true. If you ain't there in your body, you ain't there because the body is the vehicle whereby the spirit functions in a physical environment. The point of this whole story is very simple: You are the body of Christ, which means that the church is the vehicle whereby a spiritual Christ impacts a physical environment.

Our physical environment is impacted through our local churches. We exist to be the means of Christ impacting our communities. That's the purpose of the church: to be the body of Christ.

You say, "Surely when Jesus comes to live in me and I go to work, Jesus in me goes to work, and he is impacting the place." Absolutely true. But there's a great need for us to realize that we are limited by our gifts to what the expression of Christ through us can be. If we can have all the gifts, all the abilities, all the support, encouragement, interlocking, and networking coming together, then the work of Christ is much more effective. That's why I believe in the church. The church is not just a lot of individuals doing their individual independent thing, but a corporate group of people knit together to be the body of Christ.

God works out his purposes through the church

In Ephesians 3, you'll see another answer to the question "What is the purpose of the church?" Ephesians 3:10 says, "[God's] intent was that now, *through the church,* the manifold wisdom of God should be made known to the rulers and authorities in the heavenly realms" (emphasis mine). Here again is a passage that needs a lot of study. Suffice it to say that God is committed to working out his eternal purposes, and he is committed to doing it through the church! That should get you excited about being part of the church.

You mean to tell me that God's eternal purposes are being worked out in this world in a practical sense through the church? The answer is, according to Scripture, yes. Not only that, there are certain people watching the church. Did you know that there are people watching your church? You say, the IRS? Possibly. You mean other churches? Probably. You mean the papers, the media? Yes. But that's not what I'm concerned about. I'm glad they're all watching us. I hope they like what they see. I hope we're doing what we're supposed to be doing. But what really interests me is what Paul talks about here. He says that the rulers and the authorities in the heavenly places are watching the church. Why? In order that they might see his eternal purposes being worked out and his manifold wisdom being displayed.

God displays his wisdom through the church

What on earth does that mean? The word *manifold* is the same word that is used in the Greek Old Testament to describe Joseph's coat of many colors. That's what it means, literally: many colors. When you put light through a prism, you've got one ray of light. But as soon as it goes through the prism, it is broken down into all its constituent parts, the colors of the rainbow. And instead of being one beam of light, it now is many-colored. The wisdom of God is something that the rulers and authorities in the heavenly places, the angelic orders, know all about. But when the wisdom of God is refracted through the church, it is broken down into all its many varied colors, and they see how wise the wisdom of God is.

As an orthodox Jew, Paul knew that human society traditionally has been broken down and segregated. Each morning he, along with other orthodox male Jews, would recite a prayer in which he thanked God that he was not a Gentile, that he was not a slave, and that he was not a woman. That was part of the orthodox Jew's morning prayer. It gives real meaning to what Paul taught in Galatians: "In Christ there's neither Jew nor Gentile, bond nor free, male nor female, but we are all one in Christ Jesus." He was taking aim at all the traditional alienations in the society. He was taking aim at racial segregation, Jew and Gentile. He was taking aim at socioeconomic and political alienation, bond and free. He was taking aim at sexual alienation, male and female. And he was saying all those things are fundamentally wrong, and they are resolved at the Cross. For at the Cross male and female, bond and free, Jew and Gentile find their oneness; they realize that they're all the same and move into the church of Jesus Christ.

That's the theory, though the church of Jesus Christ has still a lot of work to do to put it into practice. When we see this happening, we begin to see the many-colored wisdom of God in operation. What a way to deal with the alienations of society—through the Cross, through Christ, through the church. And that's why we're here, folks, to be the body of Christ, to show the wisdom of God.

The church is to glorify God

In Ephesians 3:20-21 we have our third statement about the church: "Now to him who is able to do immeasurably more than all we ask or imagine, according to his power that is at work within us, to him be glory *in the church* and in Christ Jesus throughout all generations, for ever and ever! Amen" (emphasis mine).

Another answer to the question "What is the purpose of the church?" is "to demonstrate the glory of God." The church of Jesus Christ does not exist to demonstrate the glory of its architecture. Neither does it exist to demonstrate the glory of the academic standing of its leadership. Neither does it exist to show what sharp, smart people we are. The church of Jesus Christ exists to be the body of Christ, to show the wisdom of God, and to bring glory to God. Notice how Paul carefully talks about glory in the church and in Christ Jesus. There's no question that God is greatly glorified in Christ. And there's no question that those who believe in Christ warmly affirm that fact.

It worries me, however, that people who warmly approve of God being glorified in Christ often seem to have no desire to be part of God being glorified in the church. They don't want to commit themselves; they don't want to identify themselves with other believers.

I often come across people who say to me, "I don't believe in organized religion."

When they tell me that, I want to ask them, "Is it organized religion you're against? Is it disorganized religion you are for? . . . No . . . Oh, you want organized ir-religion. . . . No . . . Well, what is it you're opposed to?"

"I don't want to have to do what anybody else says or think what anybody else thinks. I just want to have Jesus and me on the road to heaven."

That would be fine except for the fact that Jesus is committed to building his church, and it is in the church that God's glory is to be seen, as well as in Christ and each individual Christian.

So the purpose of the church is that we might be a called-out group of people, committed to Jesus Christ, identified with the cause, working with each other, unitedly being the body, unitedly showing God's wisdom, unitedly bringing the glory. That's what I mean when I say, "I believe in the church."

The Church Is Holy

What do we mean when we say, I believe the church is holy? Do we mean that the church is perfect and sinless? Do we mean when a local church, part of the church of Jesus Christ, gathers, what is actually happening is that a group of absolutely perfect, sinless, totally holy people are found in one place? Is that what we mean? I doubt it.

If you have any doubts about that, let me remind you of the church at Corinth. If you check out what Paul said in the sixth chapter of his first letter to Corinth, he pointed out the kind of people who comprised the church there, and they were a ragtag and bobtail bunch if ever there was one. You name it, they'd done it. They had come out of every conceivable kind of bad situation, and many of them were still behaving badly indeed. They were far from perfect. They were far from sinless, but they were still called the church. So, no, when we talk about the church being holy, we do not mean that it is a tight little group of perfect people.

Some people feel that the church is holy in the sense that when the church goes off track, they split off in order to find something that is going to be right. They're going to do it right. Church history, right down through the centuries, records efforts to do that. The church has gone in a certain direction, and then a certain group decides that's not the way to go, and so they move off, and it repeats itself over and over. The attitude of these groups is, "We are the vine, and you guys are the branches." There are many instances of this. The tragedy, however, is that there always seems to be a drift away from orthodoxy into unorthodoxy, and the solution, usually, is for a group to split off and form another idealistic "perfect" group. It doesn't really solve the problem. Nevertheless, there are groups who honestly, genuinely feel that they have a corner on the truth. They think they've got it right and all the others are to be pitied or to be maligned. Is that what we mean when we say, "I believe in the holy church?" I think not.

Some members of the church have the feeling that, while it is true that the church is made up of sinful people, the church itself is holy. I've never quite understood this argument that some theologians engage in, and I won't identify them for you. It seems to me to be a modern kind of Gnosticism. The Gnostics believed that the material body was sinful and the spirit was good, and the idea seems to be that there's something holy about the church in a mystical sense, even though it is made up entirely of sinful people. That doesn't make any sense to me at all.

Let me tell you what I believe the holiness of the church is. The word *holy* comes from the word meaning "to cut." Just suppose that I am making dinner. (I assure you that this is just an illustration. If Jill were here now she would go into mild hysterics.) We're having stir-fry, and so I get all the ingredients and a sharp knife and I start chopping. I'm watching the news, however, so I accidentally chop off the end of my finger. *Cut.* The end of my finger is now separate. Because it is separate, it is really quite distinctive. In fact, it is absolutely unique, and I say, What should I do with this?

You say, This is explaining *holy?* Yes. I believe that when we talk about people being separate, people being distinct, people being saints, that is what is intended by being holy. I believe that when we talk about the church being holy, we're talking about a group of people who are a cut apart, who are separate from, who are distinctively different, who are utterly unique.

The unique founder of the church

What is it that is unique about the people who gather in the name of Christ? Three things immediately come to mind from Matthew 16:13-16. First of all, they have a unique founder. Jesus said to his disciples, "Who do people say the Son of Man is?"

They said, "Some say John the Baptist; others say Elijah; and still others Jeremiah or one of the prophets."

"But who do you say?"

And Peter came out with the answer: "You are the Christ, the Son of the living God." And he got the answer right. What is unique about the church? Its founder is unique. There is only one Son of the living God, and Jesus Christ is his name. And while there are religions and sects galore, the orthodox church, the true church of Christ, is unique in that it is founded on the person of Jesus Christ, God's only Son.

The unique foundation of the church

The church also has a unique foundation. When Peter made his confession of faith, Jesus said to him, "You are Peter, and on this rock I will build my church. And the gates of Hades shall not overthrow it." We have to admit that when Jesus said this, presumably in Aramaic, but translated in our New Testament into Greek, he was having a bit of fun. He must have been in a rare good humor that day because he was doing what the British do. He was punning. He was twisting words a little bit. So when he said, "You are Peter" (The guy was already called Simon, Simeon, and Cephas: who needs more names?) the Greek word for "Peter" is *Petros*. "You are *Petros*, and on this *petra* (rock) I will build my church." A little fun there; a little bit of humor. The trouble is, we've had problems with it ever since. *Petros* means rock. Jesus is giving Simeon, Simon, Cephas a nickname: Rocky. The point is this, that down through the centuries, people have been arguing as to whether the foundation of the church is Peter or whether the foundation of the church is Peter's confession. As usually is the case, I find myself right in the middle. It seems to me that Peter is the first one to make this confession of faith. And in a foundational sense Peter is the one on whose confession of faith the whole thing begins to build. What we're talking about in this unique society is a unique founder, the only Son of God, who calls people to personal commitment to him. That's the foundation of the church.

The unique future of the church

The church has a unique future as well. For Jesus said, "The gates of Hades will not overwhelm it." What that means is that the powers of death cannot stop it. Down through the years the church of Jesus Christ has exhibited a remarkable uniqueness, and it is this: the more it has been persecuted, the more it has grown. The powers of death do not overthrow it. In the second century, Tertullian wrote to the Roman authorities as follows, "Proceed in your career of cruelty, but do not suppose that you will thus accomplish your purpose of extinguishing the hated sect. We are like the grass which grows the more luxuriantly the oftener it is mowed." What a great picture: The blood of Christians is the seed of Christianity. The gates of hell, the powers of death will never, ever stop the church. For it will go through death into eternity, and that's what makes us holy. That's what makes us unique. We have a unique founder, a unique foundation, and a unique future.

I Believe the Church Is Catholic

Thirdly, I believe the church is catholic. Now what do I mean by that? The word *catholic* comes from the Latin and from the Greek and in both cases means "universal." At the time of the Reformation, there were those who were less than enthusiastic about the pope and what the Catholic church under the pope's leadership was doing, and so they seceded. They became Protestants; they protested what was happening. One of the things they wanted to do was put some distance between themselves and the church that had allegiance to the pope, who, in their feelings, was quite likely corrupt. So they stopped using the word *catholic* in their creed and they put in the word *Christian*—not because they didn't believe it was catholic, but just by way of differentiation. Because they did not want to identify with Rome and the Pope, they called themselves Anglo Catholic as opposed to Roman Catholic. Let's stand by the original word and it's original meaning. I believe in the catholic church. This has nothing to do with Anglo; it has nothing to do with Roman; it has nothing to do with the Reformation; it has to do with the original concept of the church.

Is the church catholic in the truer sense of the word? Absolutely yes! There's a universal need: "For all have sinned and fall short of the glory of God." There's a universal remedy: Christ died for all. There's a universal mandate: Go into all the world and preach the gospel and make disciples of all nations. And there will be a universal consummation when the church is finally gathered around the person of Christ in glory. There will be people there from every kindred and tongue and tribe and nation. The church didn't start in America. The church in its purest form is not necessarily in America. The church is found universally, catholic. And that's why I am very happy to affirm my faith today. I believe in the church, I believe it's holy, and I believe, in the true sense of the word, it's catholic. What do you believe?

MAKING IT PRACTICAL

1. What is the purpose of the church? How are we accomplishing it?

2. What do we mean when we say we believe the church is *holy?*

3. What are three things that are unique about the church?

4. Why has the church, at times, been an obstacle to belief, rather than something that attracts people and causes them to believe in God?

5. What does the word *catholic* mean? What does our belief in "the holy *catholic* church" imply about how we can view denominations, nationalities, and other differences?

12

"The Communion of Saints"

1 Corinthians 1:2

Robert Bellah, in his book *Habits of the Heart,* pointed out that one of the great strengths of American society is the freedom of the individual. But one of the great concerns in contemporary American society is that this freedom of the individual has led to rampant individualism, a lack of sense of community, and a lack of sense of commitment. There is an overriding sense in which individuals are exclusively committed to themselves. The net result, of course, is inevitable fragmenting of the society, the community of which you are a part. Sadly, this trend is to be seen in many aspects of the church of Jesus Christ too. There is an individualism about our spiritual experience. Not infrequently, we find that people want spirituality, but not in terms of the church of Jesus Christ, not in terms of the communion of saints.

Lenny Bruce, the insightful comedian, on one occasion said this: "People are leaving the churches and returning to God." By that he meant many people are dissatisfied with the whole concept of the church and see no need for it at all, but are interested in a spiritual experience.

It is the clear teaching of Scripture that one of the fundamental aspects of spiritual life is the communion of saints. What are saints? And what is communion? I want to talk about saints above and saints below. And if you're wondering a little bit about those two expressions, let me quote you one of my favorite poems: "To dwell above with saints I love, to me that will be glory. To dwell below with saints I know, well, that's another story." We do have to dwell with saints above. We do have to dwell with saints below. And the communion of saints incorporates both.

Saints Alive

Who are the saints? We're all familiar with old-fashioned Bibles that have the Gospels according to Saint Matthew, Saint Mark, Saint Luke, and Saint John. And we say the saints are the evangelists. Some of us may come from traditions that understand that in the early days when someone was martyred, they were regarded as being extraspecial believers and, not infrequently, the place where they were buried was marked by a building in which Christians began to meet. The name of that martyr would then be applied to the church. This tradition is being carried on, so we have the Cathedral of St. John, St. Mark's Episcopal Church, etc. Those of us who come from a Catholic background are probably quite familiar with the system of beatification and canonization. Often the idea people have of saints is that they are either martyrs or people who, through their intercession, have performed specific miracles or have been known for their heroic virtue and have been canonized by the church. But is that all that we mean when we talk about saints? I think not.

Let me refer you to 1 Corinthians 1:2, where Paul is addressing "the church of God in Corinth, to those sanctified in Christ Jesus and called to be holy, together with all those everywhere who call on the name of our Lord Jesus Christ—their Lord and ours." The Greek word translated "saints" is *hagioi,* which comes from the Greek word for holy. It is related to the word *sanctified.* So when we read that his letter is addressed to those sanctified in Christ, called holy, it is perfectly legitimate, as some of the older translations say, to say that this letter is addressed to the church at Corinth, to those set apart in Christ Jesus, called saints.

178

Saints were the ordinary people of the fellowship at Corinth. When we think, therefore, in terms of saints, we think of those who are, first of all, called to be the church of God in a specific geographic location. It bears repeating that church is not somewhere you go; church is something you are. When you get individuals who are called to relationship to Christ, they then should appropriately come together as a recognizable, visible group of people, recognizably a church. We are called as saints to be the church.

We are called to be sanctified. That means we are uniquely set apart as belonging to Christ and committed to his service. We are called to be identified with Christ as we call on the name of the Lord Jesus Christ. Every time we use the word *Christian,* we take the name of Christ upon ourselves. Every time we call ourselves the church, we remind ourselves that the etymological root of the English word *church* is *kuriakon* or *kuriake*, which means "belonging to the Lord." So, when we are called to identify with Christ, to be set apart for Christ, to be uniquely the church of Christ, we are, in the strict sense of the word, saints.

So look around your church, and you will see that the place is full of saints. Some of them will probably become very deferential about that and say, "I'm no saint." What they mean by that is that they reserve the right to be less than they ought to be. "I'm no saint, and he or she is certainly no saint," we may say (referring to our spouses, of course). But strictly speaking, if you have been called by Christ to be part of his church, to identify with him, to call upon his name, and to be set apart for his service, you're a saint. And you'd better believe it.

If you look further into the epistles to the Corinthians, you'll find some surprising information. In 1 Corinthians 6:9-10, the apostle Paul, writing to the saints, says this to them:

Do you not know that the wicked will not inherit the kingdom of God? Do not be deceived: Neither the sexually immoral nor idolaters nor adulterers nor male prostitutes nor homosexual offenders nor thieves nor the greedy

179

nor drunkards nor slanderers nor swindlers will inherit the kingdom of God.

That's a very straightforward statement, a powerful, challenging, condemning statement. Those kinds of people will not inherit the kingdom of God. Then he says (verse 11), dramatically and remarkably addressing the saints, "and that is what some of you were." In other words, these saints that constituted the church at Corinth had been sexually immoral, idolaters, adulterers, prostitutes, homosexual offenders, thieves, greedy, drunkards, slanderers, swindlers; what a motley crew, engaging in all kinds of overt activity in dynamic opposition to all that God had said. That's who the saints were.

What in the world happened to them? I'm glad you asked. Look what he goes on to say: "But you were washed, you were sanctified, you were justified in the name of the Lord Jesus Christ and by the Spirit of our God." What had happened to these people is that when they were called, they had been thoroughly converted. Because of their behavior, they were not participants in the kingdom of God, make no mistake about it. It is necessary for those who engage in behavior that is in opposition to all that God has required (and that's all of us) to recognize that we must respond to the call of God. We must identify with Christ as Savior and Lord and be thoroughly converted through the activity of the Holy Spirit in our lives. Then we become participants in the kingdom that, prior to conversion, we were banished from. We will then be justified. We will then be saints, called and converted.

Notice, however, that the apostle Paul took great pains to point out repeatedly to those early believers that if they had become saints in this strict sense of the word, then they were challenged to live in newness of life. In Ephesians 5:3 he says: "Among you there must not be even a hint of sexual immorality, or of any kind if impurity, or of greed, because these are improper for God's *hagioi* [these are improper for God's saints; these are improper for God's holy people]."

What then is a saint? A saint is a very ordinary person who, recognizing his or her sin—overt and gross or covert and respectable—has come to the point of repentance and faith in the Lord Jesus, has sensed his call to belong to him and to publicly identify with him, and has become part of the body of believers. As a result of that, they have responded to the call, they have been thoroughly converted through the work of the Spirit in their lives, and they are responding to the challenge to live in newness of life. That's a saint. When we talk about the communion of saints, when we profess faith in the communion of saints, that's what we should be thinking about.

Sharing our relationship with Christ

Next is the idea of communion. If you were to go to Greece this summer, you would discover that they would be speaking modern Greek. If, however, you read some of the classical Greek authors, you would find that they wrote classical Greek. However, in between those, there was another kind of Greek that was the Greek of the era in which Christ lived. *Koinē* Greek was common Greek, the language of the common people, the language of the marketplace. *Koinē* means "common." *Koinōnia,* a word that comes from *koinē,* means communion, fellowship, partnership, relationship. It has the root idea of sharing or having in common. So when we talk of the communion of saints, what we're talking about is all these people, called, converted, challenged to live in newness of life, in some way sharing in fellowship, partnership, relationship. Sharing is the key idea.

What do we share? Paul, writing to the Corinthians, says, "God has called us into fellowship with his Son, Jesus Christ our Lord." What this means is that when I respond to the call of Christ and I'm converted, then I enjoy sharing my life with the Son. In simple terms it means this: As I make my life available to him, he makes his life available to me. That is the most simple statement and the most profound truth. I'm called to fellowship with the Son.

But when I realize that every other believer who has fellowship with the Son shares the same life that I share, I begin to discover that there is a horizontal dimension to my faith as well as a vertical. We share a common life. We acknowledge a common Lord. He is fundamental to our spiritual experience, yours and mine. That means, therefore, there will be many differences of understanding; there will be many differences of social, political, and economic standing. But these will all be secondary, for we've all been called—every single saint—to share our lives with the Son.

Not only that, when we have the benediction to our church service, we "proclaim the peace to each other." This benediction begins, "May the grace of our Lord Jesus and the love of God, the fellowship [the *koinōnia*] of the Holy Spirit . . . " What does fellowship in the Spirit mean? The Bible tells us that the greatest dynamic in the world today is the dynamic working of the Spirit of God, opening blind eyes, turning people from darkness to light, creating in them newness of life. It is nothing less than the Spirit of him who raised up Christ from the dead. He now dwells in the humblest believer. Every single one of them. So now I begin to discover that the communion of saints is not only communion with the Son; it is communion in the Spirit. The startling thing about it is this: The same Spirit who indwells me, indwells every other believer.

Therefore, it ought to be hypothetically possible for Christians to agree. For it is obvious that we acknowledge the same Lord and are motivated by the same Spirit. The Lord is not going to be against himself, and the Spirit is not going to militate against himself. Of course, there is another factor here, and that is that residual sinfulness and selfishness within us. There are different aspects to truth, and some of us will see one side of it and some of us will see the other. But when we enjoy the communion of saints, we concentrate on the things we have in common and recognize that other things are of a secondary nature. We enjoy common life in the Son. We enjoy common experience in the Spirit.

When I was growing up as a teenager, I started preaching, and I was invited to go to a lot of little churches around the area. A rather select, rather exclusive group that I'd been brought up in did not approve, and so some of the elders of that group sat me down, including my father. And they said, "Stuart, we don't approve of you going to meet with these people. Why do you want to go to them?"

Being brash and somewhat impertinent, I said, "I'm practicing for heaven."

"What do you mean?"

I replied, "When you get to heaven, you won't know anybody, because you think you're the only ones going there, but I've discovered all kinds of people, in all kinds of little churches, who don't agree with you on some points . . . "

If I'd known enough, I'd have told them, "They all fellowship with the Son, and they all have fellowship in the Spirit, and this is the essence of the communion of saints."

Sharing in communion

We share at the supper as well. We're all familiar to some extent or the other with that precious aspect of Christian worship, when we take the bread and wine and we share it with each other. What are we doing? As far as the communion of saints is concerned, we're saying, As I take this bread and drink this wine, I am simply saying that I feed on Christ and the merits of his broken body, the merits of his shed blood, because I am a sinner and he is my only hope. But that's only part of it. For the bread and the wine are then passed to the next person, and you know what happens? They do the same thing and say the same thing. So what's our communion now? It's a communion of sinners saved by grace.

If we can begin to look at our relationships with each other on that basis, we will realize that we're nothing more than sinners, but we're nothing less than saved by grace. That ought to be the basis of our relationship to each other. There's no need to look down on anybody: How can a sinner look down on a sinner? But there's also no need to excuse behavior that is not becoming to saints, for we have the power to be different and to live differently. We should be looking to each other and encouraging each other, and that's what we say when we share the supper together. Communion of saints means sharing with the saints.

When Paul wrote to Titus, he talked about the common faith. When Jude wrote his Epistle, he talked about common salvation, and when those early Christians gathered together in Jerusalem, it says repeatedly, "They were together and they had things in common." There was a practical outworking. They realized they were all sinners. They realized they all acknowledged Christ. They realized they were all saved by grace and indwelt by the Spirit. They realized they had all been set apart to serve Christ and be uniquely identified with him. They knew all this, and therefore they looked at each other and said, "Why in the world are we pulling in opposite directions? Why aren't we getting together and collectively being together?" It's the easiest thing in the world for Christians to find points on which they disagree and major on them. The difficult thing is what we're supposed to do: find what we have in common—communion—nurture it, and commit ourselves to it. For years we've been saying, "I believe in the holy catholic or the holy Christian church, the communion of saints." But have we really been saying, I know what a saint is, and I know what the communion of saints is, and I'm committed to it?

Saints Above

Let's turn our attention now to saints above. You can join all kinds of organizations down here on earth, and I suppose many of you have done that. The problem with them is that when you die or when other members die, that's the end of the relationship. There's a uniqueness, however, about the church of Jesus Christ or the communion of saints, and it is this: Death doesn't terminate it. There is, in a very real sense, a communion, a sharing of those down here with those, if I can speak spatially, up there. There is a relationship between those who are still alive in the body and those who are alive in Christ.

People often ask me, "Are your parents still alive?" And I say, "Very much alive." They say, "Oh, really? Where do they live—in England?" I say, "No, in heaven." I have a real sense of oneness with them. Now, before you get alarmed, I do *not* mean I'm into channeling. What I mean is that we share a common Lord and a common salvation, and my parents just got there ahead of me. So they should, as they started before me. But they are entering into more and more of the salvation, which was their birthright in Christ, than I have yet had the opportunity to do. One of these days, I'll pop off and I'll go to glory. I'll be absent from the body, present with the Lord. But you and I will still have communion. We'll share a common Lord, a common life. I'll just be a little bit ahead of you, preparing a nice place for you. That is the communion that goes on in the uniqueness of the communion of saints.

The Bible talks about those who have entered into their rest. It talks about those same holy ones, *hagioi*, saints, coming with Christ at his return in great glory. Some translate, quite accurately, *hagioi* as "angels," and others legitimately translate it as "saints." And so theologians have a great time debating whether it's angels or saints who will come with him at his return. And I have the solution for you: It's both. I see no reason at all why he shouldn't bring the whole caboose with him. When Christ comes in his return, his glorious return, he will bring the saints and the angels, and the mass choirs today will pale into insignificance, and all those with whom we have communion will say, "You'll just love it here." The communion of saints.

There's another aspect to it, however, and it is this. Those whom we love and those who've gone before have joined with those who've gone before whom we never knew. For instance, read Hebrews 11 sometime: a great catalog of heroes of the faith. They are a wonderful bunch, many of them mentioned by name, many of them anonymous. However, in Hebrews 12:1 the writer goes on to say: "Since we are surrounded by such a great cloud of witnesses . . .

185

let us run with perseverance the race marked out for us." It is a dramatic picture of those who have gone on before, the heroes of the faith, who are now the saints above in the presence of the Lord. They are sitting in the stands in the arena, and down on the floor of the arena the marathon race is being run. And those who've gone before, the saints above, are in the stands.

And guess where we are? Running the race. So says the writer of the Hebrews. Given who handed the baton on to us, given the heroes of the faith, given the glorious company of martyrs, given those saints with whom we have communion, we need to see them as an incentive and follow their example. Recognize that we are part of all that they started, and run with perseverance the marathon race you enrolled in, and don't quit.

Saints Below

But then, of course, there are saints below. "To dwell below with saints I know—well, that's another story." What's the other story? If it is true that you and I are really saints in the strict sense of the word, and if it is true that we have a sharing with those who've gone before, what about the here and now? We're supposed to have a special relationship here, and the three key words are *fellowship, partnership,* and *relationship.*

Acts 2:42, speaking of those new believers in Jerusalem, says, "They devoted themselves to . . . the fellowship," the *koinōnia.* They were clearly identifiable as people whose lives were devoted to some other clearly identifiable people. They needed the support, the nurture, the encouragement, the reproof, the correction, and the instruction of righteousness. Those saints devoted themselves to a clearly identifiable fellowship. The fellowship could count on them. They could count on the fellowship. Everybody knew it, and therein lay much of their spiritual security.

Let me say to you, quite frankly, this is one of the great weaknesses of many people who sit around the edges of our churches today. There is no devotion of their lives to the lives of other people. And if that is the case, there's a blind spot in their under-standing of the communion of saints. There should be devotion to the fellowship. The apostle Paul, writing to the Corinthians and the Philippians, used the word *koinōnia* in another sense. He thanked the people there for their partnership in the gospel. God had called him to head off into the wide blue yonder, to have a ministry that they could never have, to which they had never been called, and he'd gone to do it. But the people in Macedonia and the people in Achaia had said, "We will be your partners. We will share in this ministry. We can't go, but you can. This is what we'll do: we'll commit ourselves to prayer; we'll commit ourselves to your inter-est; we'll commit ourselves to financial support. We will be part-ners in the ministry."

I was talking to somebody the other day who was starting a new ministry, and this is what he told me. "I am looking for ten commit-ted men."

I said, "Why ten committed men?"

He said, "I'm looking for ten committed men who will commit one tenth of their salary to my ministry, which will then enable me to live among them at the level they live."

I calculated, and I figured that if they did that, he'd be slightly ahead, because they'd be living on 90 percent and he'd be living on 100 percent. But I didn't point that out to him. Mathematically he needed a slight adjustment, but what a powerful thought. Ten peo-ple gathering around another person and saying, "We are partners in this ministry, and you can count on us. We will share realistically with you. We can count on you to minister; you can count on us to be your partners." Think of the possibilities! That's the communion of saints—devoted to the fellowship, sharing in partnership.

Finally, John talks in his first Epistle about us having fellowship with God. And then he says, surprisingly, that this fellowship with God is shown in the fellowship that we have with each other. In other words, it isn't enough just to say, "I have fellowship with God." For if I have fellowship with God, I will have fellowship with his people.

Then he explains what happens when we have real fellowship with his people. He says we walk in the light, meaning that in our relationships with each other, we relate according to the principles of Scripture. If the Scripture shows me something that is wrong in my relationship with somebody else, or if somebody else sees something that is wrong in my relationship with them, then if they're walking in the light and truly having fellowship with the Father and with me, they will come to me or I will go to them. Then we will sit down together and put right what's wrong with our relationship. If the light shows something that is wrong, I will confess it, and the blood of Jesus Christ will cleanse me from it. Quite frankly, the church of Jesus Christ tends to be weak at this point of the communion of saints. We tend to ignore, gloss over, talk around, and talk behind instead of walking in the light and enjoying fellowship with each other, which demonstrates our fellowship with him. So, it's the easiest thing in the world to say, "I believe in the communion of saints," but it demands a whole new lifestyle to live out that statement. Do you believe in the communion of saints?

MAKING IT PRACTICAL

1. What does the Greek word for "saints" mean? Who are "the saints"?

2. What do all the saints have in common?

3. What does "the communion of saints" mean?

4. Where do you see communion? What effect does it have on the surrounding world?

5. What are the demands of belief in "the communion of the saints"? Does your lifestyle show that you believe in "the communion of the saints"? How?

13

"The Forgiveness of Sins"

Luke 24:47

In his commissioning of the disciples, the Lord Jesus told them that repentance and forgiveness of sins would be preached in all nations. This is an integral part of Christian experience—to repent and know forgiveness. And it is an integral part of the Christian mandate and message that we go out into the world and present forgiveness and repentance. However, we immediately run into some problems, because we're not always taking this truth of the forgiveness of sins seriously enough.

The Bible certainly does. No fewer than seven different words are translated "forgiveness" in the Bible. Three of them are in the Old Testament from the Hebrew, and four of them are from the New Testament in the Greek. The most common of these words, *Aphesis,* means literally "sending away or letting go." Forgiveness means sending away responsibility for sin, letting people go from their accountability of their sin, no longer holding them accountable for their guilt, their sin, and their shame. That is the basic idea of forgiveness.

Having said that, however, we need to look further into it. I want to suggest three things to you. First of all, forgiveness requires recognizing. By that I mean we need to recognize what we have done that needs to be forgiven. Clearly, if we have no consciousness of wrongdoing, there will be no interest whatsoever in being forgiven for this wrongdoing. Secondly, forgiveness requires repenting to the extent that we're aware of the depth of our wrongdoing; we will be open to a genuine kind of repentance. And that is an integral part of forgiveness. The mandate was that repentance and forgiveness of sins be preached. And then, in addition to that, forgiveness requires receiving. It is possible to recognize my sin and to repent of my sin, but not to be in an open, humble attitude where I'll be prepared to receive what God offers me by his grace, to live in the goodness of that forgiveness.

Forgiveness Requires Recognizing

Anselm, the ancient archbishop of Canterbury, said, "You have not yet considered the heavy weight sin is." I find that to be one of the most provocative statements I've read in a long time. And I think it's a statement that is appropriate to our society at the present time. We have not yet considered the heavy weight that sin is. One of the reasons for that, of course, is the influence of many of the social and behavioral sciences on our thinking. Frequently, people are more influenced by what an anthropologist, a sociologist, or a psychologist says than what God has said in his Word.

Psychologists have discovered, I think quite rightly, that it is possible to modify people's behavior. So, for instance, when our children are growing up, we know how to give them positive or negative reinforcement. We would say to our children, "If you are a very good boy when I come home, I will do this, that, or the other." This is called bribing or positive reinforcement. And their behavior was modified. Conversely, we would say to them, "If you do such-and-such a thing again, I'm going to have to spank you." Now you must realize that this never happened with my children. Jill's, yes, but never with my children. And it was necessary for us on rare occasions to say to them, "If you do that again, we will have to deal rather firmly with you." Eventually they got the message, and they stopped doing those things. Thus, behavior modification through the application of certain negatives.

There's a saying in England that when it comes to responding to what social scientists or behavioral scientists have discovered, there's a "nothing buttery" approach to it. By that we mean that when we look at what the scientists are discovering about human behavior, there is a tendency for them, having made their discovery, to say that human beings are this and there's *nothing but* that to be seen. In other words, when it comes to human behavior, it is simply a matter of positive or negative reinforcement; it is learned behavior, and it's nothing but that.

It's at that point that the Christian has to take issue with the social scientist or the behavioral scientist, because the Scriptures say certainly there is a power called sin. And it isn't just a matter of behavior modification. It is a matter of dealing with this thing called sin as well.

Or look at it another way. There are people in our world who are convinced of the fact that the great need in our society is education. They believe that if we just educate people, then they will have the facts, they will know how to behave, and they will behave correctly. Notice the logic. If they have the facts, they will know the facts. And if they know the facts they will know how to behave, and if they know how to behave, they will.

Somewhere there's a flaw. No question about it: If you are educated with facts, you're better off than not knowing. There's no question about it that if you know the facts, you know the behavior that is appropriate. But it is a false assumption that if we know what the right thing to do is, we will do it. It just doesn't happen that way. The Christian is perfectly open to education, perfectly open to people discovering the facts, but he or she is never foolish enough to assume that because a person knows what is right and good and true, he will automatically do it. He knows enough about human nature, and he's got enough theology in his head to know that people don't necessarily do what they know is the right thing to do.

It isn't a case of simply needing an education. Yes, let's discover what education can tell us, but we must not necessarily assume that we will do what is right, because there's another factor—sin—that must be reckoned in.

Because some people discovered how pigeons behaved and some others discovered how dogs behaved, they decided that there's a large similarity between the way they behave and the way human beings behave. Some people have even come to the point, as did Dr. Desmond Morris, the zoologist, of saying that man is simply a naked ape, *"nothing but*tery." Well, it's true that we're very similar to animals. It's true that our behavior is not dissimilar at times. Sometimes the animals even stoop to our standards of behavior. It is true that physiologically there are marked similarities. But the "nothing buttery" won't do. For to simply say we are nothing but sophisticated animals negates what the Bible says about our unique humanity and the fact that we have a power of sin operating within us.

Mark Twain, of all people, got it right. He said, "Man is the only animal that blushes or needs to." He recognized that we're certainly related to the animal kingdom but there's something about us that needs to blush. And we have that capability. So let's look and try to see what Anselm was talking about when he said, "You have not yet considered the heavy weight sin is." We won't consider individual sins, but rather sin in principle. And in order to do that, we need to understand how humanity is designed.

The beginning chapters of Genesis tell us that man is created to depend upon God. In the same way that birds are free as they fly in the air and fish are free as they swim in the sea, so man is free when he lives in dependence upon God. If the air is the domain of the bird and the water is the domain of the fish, dependence upon God is the domain of man. We need to recognize that that is how we are made. We need to recognize that we were created to delight in the Lord and to bring him delight. And in addition to that, we were created to discover who the Lord is and to discover and to do his will. And I think it would be true to say that to the extent we are prepared to depend on him, delight in him, and discover him and his will and do it, we will fulfill our humanity.

Over against a consideration of humanity's constitution, we need to recognize a gross contradiction: that mankind refuses fellowship with God. We were created to depend upon God and to delight in God, but for some reason we don't really want that. We don't mind God being locked up in the church. We don't mind visiting him on occasion, somewhat like a sick relative in a nursing home, but we're not too sure that we want to take God wherever we go. Do we want to take him into the business, into the entertainment world, into our relationships? We're not too sure that we want God watching what we love to watch and reading what we love to read and gazing at what we love to do. We recognize that there's a time when we'd like God very much to take a back seat, and fellowship with him is something that we refuse with regularity.

In other words, we want to reserve the right to paddle our own canoe, to determine our own destiny, to do our own thing. Although we are told that all our resources are really God's, we still resist this concept of handling our resources as stewards for him. There is a buillt-in, intuitive rejection of the concept of divine ownership of our lives. You see, there's something about us that, while we know we're created to depend and delight and discover, we insist on refusing and rejecting and rebelling. And we need to ask ourselves a serious question: What is it about us that makes us like that? Well, Anselm had the answer: It's the heavy weight of sin. And we need to consider it.

Consider not only sin in principle; consider sin in practice. A little boy and his mother were talking. His mother said, "It's time to get ready for Sunday school."

He said, "I'm not going."

She said, "Oh yes you are."

He said, "I don't want to go."

She said, "I don't recollect asking you if you wanted to go. You're going."

"Why do I have to go to Sunday school?"

"To learn to be a good little boy."

And here's where the little boy demonstrates tremendous insight into human makeup. He answered, "I already know how to be a better little boy than I want to be."

All right now, have your laugh, and then think about it. What is it about little boys that enables them to know how to be better little boys than they want to be? The same thing that allows big boys and girls to know how to be a whole lot better than they want to be. And we have to have an answer to that remarkable phenomenon. What is it? Well, Anselm had the answer. It's the heavy weight that sin is. We need to consider that there is a deep root of sin within us.

In Romans chapter 7, Paul talks about sin from his own personal experience. He says there were lots of times that he wanted to do good things and really had the desire to do them—and finished up not doing them. And there were lots of times that he knew there were some bad things that he ought to give up, and he promised he would give them up and then found he'd picked them up again. In the end he comes to a point of tremendous despair and talks about being a wretched man: "Who's going to deliver me?"

I get two pictures from what he's saying here. First, this root of sin within us tends to destroy us. We often talk about people being self-destructive, and in extreme cases that is absolutely true. But isn't it true that all of us recognize the strange discrepancy between knowing and doing, believing and performing, desiring and discovering? Isn't it true that there's something spiritually self-destructive about that? It's as if there's a power that's bigger than we are. As Paul would put it, "The good that I would, I do not. And the evil that I would not, that I do."

Not only is it a dynamic that destroys; it's almost like a disease that debilitates. If the dynamic pushes us to do things that in our better moments we don't want to do, the disease robs us of the ability to do the thing that in our nobler moments we long to do. And therein lies the problem. If sin is the root, sins are the fruit. And this fruit is demonstrated in a wide variety of ways.

How is it that we can be perfectly happy for long stretches of time being basically indifferent to who God is and to what his calling is for us? Is it true that to a large extent we can live our lives relatively contentedly without giving any real consideration to what it is that God wants to do?

I submit to you that it is possible for us to do that. If you're anything like me, that's the way I tend to operate. And it is disconcerting to me because I am very aware of a tendency to radical indifference to the things that really matter. I can get myself totally committed to secondary issues and be blatantly, casually, callously indifferent to primary issues, and that's the nature of my sin. Radical indifference. Radical independence.

If it is true that I am created as a human being and designed so that my humanity can only ultimately be lived out in terms of dependence upon God, and I know it, what is it about me that insists on acting independently? God says, "Do this." I say, "I don't want to do it." God says, "Stop doing that." I say, "But I like doing it." God says, "Go here." And I say, "I don't particularly want to go there." Why is it that, granted I give an academic nod to the fact that I'm obviously created totally dependent, I still commit myself to radical independence? That's the nature of my sin. Is it true that you and I have a tendency to interfere with the purposes of God in our own lives? And as a result of that, do we have a marked ability to interfere in the purposes of God? It could well be that I not only hinder the purposes of God in my life, but I am a detrimental influence on the purposes of God in somebody else's life. Is that true or not? Of course it's true. And that is the nature of our sin. Anselm was right. We have not yet considered the heavy weight that sin is.

But now we need to consider sin in perspective. Let me remind you of the story of the Prodigal Son, or the Gracious Father, or the Prodigal Sons. I've heard it called all these things. The father divided his inheritance between his two sons. One stayed home and grumbled, and the other one took off and spent it and blew it—totally messed up, hit rock bottom—and them came to himself and decided he was going home. On his way home, he rehearsed a little speech: "I have sinned against heaven and against you and I am no more worthy."

The primary perspective of sin is that we have sinned against heaven. Since the Jews were reluctant to use the word *God,* they would use other words for God. So, for instance, Matthew's gospel, which was written for the Jews, talks about the kingdom of heaven, which means the kingdom of God. So when this Jewish young man says, "I have sinned against heaven," he's saying, in effect, I have sinned against God.

We have not considered the heavy weight that sin is. You know why? Because frequently we subscribe to the popular notion that it doesn't matter what you do as long as you don't hurt anybody. That is a widely held belief. What if God has told you not to do it? What if God, knowing that you depend upon him, knowing that he reaches out in love and grace to you, knowing that he has given you a covenant relationship, what if God sits up in heaven and sees you flatly refusing to do what he says? What if he sees you totally ignoring him, trampling his covenant underfoot, and treating his love and grace with utter disdain? That is sin against God. And it may be hypothetically possible to do what you're going to do without hurting anybody, though it's doubtful. But if God has given you principles and when you disobey those principles, you sin against heaven, and that is the major perspective of sin.

Second, there is the sociological aspect to sin as well. And while we can grant hypothetically that it may be possible for us to sin without hurting anybody else, it's rare. We live so inextricably bound up in other people's lives that what we do has a ripple effect. As the Bible puts it, the sins of the fathers are even visited on the third and fourth generations. Our sins are against another person.

Third, our sins are against ourselves. There is a tremendous sense of shame and guilt that will make many people say, "I am just no longer worthy." Some time ago I read a book that extolled the virtues of free love and wife-swapping and all that sort of thing.

While this book advocated this kind of lifestyle and said that it was mature and free, it was quite open and frank in saying that the major problem the people have in this kind of lifestyle is an overwhelming sense of guilt. If only they could get rid of a sense of guilt, and if only they could get rid of a sense of shame, they really would be free. But you see, the problem is this: It is the heavy weight that sin is. For sin is not only against heaven and against another person; it's against myself in the long run. The load of guilt and the load of shame won't go away. So if we are to be interested at all in forgiveness, it starts with recognizing what a heavy weight sin is.

Forgiveness Requires Repentance

Then there's the second stage. The Lord Jesus mandated to his disciples that repentance and forgiveness be preached in all nations. And so quite understandably the second aspect is that forgiveness requires repenting. There are various levels of repentance. Some people will repent of their sins when the consequences of their sins catch up with them; some people will repent of their sins when they're caught in the act of sinning. In actual fact, that kind of repentance is just being sorry that they're suffering for what they've done or sorry that they're now going to live with the consequences of what they've done. It is infantile repentance.

Notice what Job said after the long debates and discussions with his so-called friends. After he'd defended himself against all kinds of accusations, he said to God, "My eyes have seen you; therefore, I repent." I submit to you that while there is a kind of repentance that is sorry for what I've done because it is now hurting me, or sorry for what I've done because I'm ashamed that I've been caught, or sorry for what I've done because now the consequences are being heaped upon me, that's not really the repentance we're talking about. The repentance that we're talking about is the repentance that recognizes we have sinned against heaven, and we have a vision of God, of holiness, of righteousness and truth, and we see ourselves as shabby before it.

Isaiah had a vision that led to repentance. He saw the holiness of God and was utterly overwhelmed with his own sinfulness. Peter was fishing one day and the Lord told him to cast on one side of the boat, and he got a record catch. Being the intrepid and skilled fisherman, he did a most remarkable thing. Instead of making sure he got the catch on board, he fell at Jesus' feet and said, "Depart from me, for I am a sinful man." He had a vision of the total holiness of Christ.

And Paul had a vision of the risen Lord. And the vision of the risen Lord, according to what he said in Romans chapter 2, led him to an understanding that it is the goodness and kindness of God that leads to repentance. I submit to you that true repentance doesn't come when my sin catches up with me or I have to live with the consequence of what I've done. True repentance comes when I have a vision of the holiness, the otherness, the goodness, the kindness, and the graciousness of God, and I see how I have trodden his grace underfoot, and my heart breaks. That's repentance.

I'm afraid that if Archbishop Anselm were to come back to our society today, he would say even more forcefully. "You've not yet considered the heavy weight sin is." As a result of that, there's shallow repentance, and as a result of that, there's inadequate understanding of forgiveness. But I want you to notice the alternative visions that people have.

In Luke chapter 18 the Lord Jesus tells the story about two men going to the temple; one is absolutely full of himself. In fact, it says rather humorously that the Pharisee stood up and prayed about himself. That's great. He's supposedly praying to God, but his vision is of himself: "God, I thank you that I am not like other men—robbers, evildoers, and adulterers—or even like this tax collector. I fast twice a week and give a tenth of all I get" (verses 11-12). In other words, "God, aren't you lucky to have me on your side? What would you have done without me?" The tax collector standing nearby was beating on his chest and praying a very simple prayer, "God have mercy on me, a sinner" (verse 13). And the Lord Jesus' commentary is devastating. The first guy who goes and prays about himself does not go away justified. The little guy who goes in, conscious of his sin, repents, and then humbly asks to be forgiven, goes away forgiven. You see, the first man was full of his own self-importance, and he had no vision of his sin. And with no vision of his sin, he saw no need for repentance and knew nothing of forgiveness.

The Lord Jesus tells the story in Luke chapter 12 of a man who's totally self-indulgent, having done well in business. This man says, "I'm going to take life easy; I'm going to eat, drink, and be merry." Does that ring a bell? He is totally absorbed with himself, totally wrapped up in this world, totally oblivious to the things of eternity, the things of God, and the things of righteousness and truth. He is simply captivated by his self-indulgence. He is utterly oblivious to his own sinfulness, and therefore, he has no concept of repentance and no experience of forgiveness. The world is full of the self-important, the self-indulgent, and the self-sufficient. Their vision goes no further than themselves. They have no vision of God.

Forgiveness Requires Receiving

I suppose it would be possible to admit and recognize my sin and be sorry for my sin and still not live in the conscious enjoyment of being forgiven. A person might have an inadequate understanding of the fact of what David said: "Blessed is he whose transgressions are forgiven." And what that means is this, that there is forgiveness, but only God can forgive sins. The question is, Will he? and the answer is, Yes, he will. Out of grace—not because of our merit, but solely because of his grace—he reaches out and offers us forgiveness.

But everybody who has got a brain knows there's no such thing as a free lunch. Oh, it may be totally free to you if you're the recipient, but somebody footed the bill. Grace is free, and Christ footed the bill. The principle of forgiveness is that it is offered by the grace of God and provided by the cross of Christ. Sin is such a heavy weight that God decided that the only way it could be dealt with was for him, in the person of his Son, to bear our sins in his body on the cross and purchase forgiveness for us. Offered by the grace of God, provided by the cross of Christ, forgiveness must be received by humbly receptive people.

I went to see my little grandson Danny one day. I took him some children's books Jill had written. And when I got there, it was a little sad. He should have been very excited about them, but he wasn't at all because his hands were loaded with stuff: a blanket, a toy, a fire engine, and a sticky bun. So when I said, "Danny, I've got some books for you," he couldn't do anything with them. His hands were too full to receive.

The tragedy for many people is this, that God in grace offers them forgiveness and Christ on the cross has purchased them forgiveness, but they're not in a fit attitude to receive it because they're clutching on to their sticky buns, they're hanging on to their toys, and they're keeping to themselves their security blankets. Those things are called sin. Have you considered what a heavy weight sin is? Have you considered the immensity of divine grace, the wonder of Christ's love, and the glory of being forgiven? Do you believe in the forgiveness of sins?

MAKING IT PRACTICAL

1. What other belief is implicit in belief in forgiveness of sins? Why is this necessary to an understanding of forgiveness?

2. What three things are required of the person who is forgiven?

3. How have the behavioral sciences influenced our ideas of sin and forgiveness?

4. What might we be holding on to that prevents us from being able to accept forgiveness?

14

"The Resurrection of the Body"

1 Corinthians 15:35

I want you all to check that you've brought your bodies to your reading of this book. Is there anybody who did not bring their bodies? Come to think of it, how would you? You can't. But in actual fact, you didn't bring your body. Because it isn't that you have a body, a soul, and spirit so much as you *are* body and spirit and soul. Clearly our bodies are a major part of what we are. They may be the part of us that we're most familiar with because we can see them. Some of us wish we couldn't see them, and some us wish there wasn't as much of them to see. Some of us would like to reshape what we see. Have you ever noticed how enthusiastically so many people are caring for their bodies right now? I mean, food is in. People are really concerned about what they're going to eat. What puzzles me is why God made all this food for us to eat that is so bad for us. Evidently, either he didn't understand or we haven't quite got it, or maybe we just eat too much of it or don't get the balance right.

Have you noticed how many people are really into fitness? This afternoon I went for a run, hoping it might help a bit. And fashion, what we hang on our bodies, is quite important to some people. You can tell that by the amount of money people put into it, the way they sort of sail in and you can't help noticing. We take a lot of notice of our bodies.

But I've got news for you. Well, maybe it isn't news. Your body will not last forever; it is going to disintegrate. Now don't be alarmed; I don't mean that little bits are going to drop off. What I mean is that it's going to get older, and you won't be able to do with it the things that you used to do. Eventually—and I hate to mention this—you'll die. And then your body returns to the dust out of which, surprisingly, it was made. But our bodies are important.

I'll tell you what makes them wonderfully important: When you die, that's not the end of you. You move into eternity, where you'll have a new body, a body as ideally suited for eternity as your body now is suited for time. It will be as ideally suited for the limitless regions of space as your body is ideally suited for the restrictions of earth. Please don't ask me to describe it because I don't know. We don't have that information. But the Bible teaches and Christians believe in the resurrection of the body or the giving of a new body after we die.

We need, therefore, to understand three things: the body, death, and resurrection. And then I think we'll understand what we mean by the resurrection of the body.

Understanding the Body

First of all, let's look at the design of the body. Psalm 139 has a lovely old expression: we are "fearfully and wonderfully made." When we understand our bodies and how God made our bodies (and notice I said how *God* made our bodies) then we will realize they are so wonderful that we will have a tremendous sense of awe and wonder and amazement. And as we learn more and more about our bodies, we learn more and more about the wonders of God and the wonders of his creation.

Fearfully and wonderfully made

Your body is a miracle. If you want to go out and make yourself a body, here's a list of things you'll need: fifty-eight pounds of oxygen, two ounces of salt, fifty quarts of water, three pounds of calcium, and twenty-four pounds of carbon. Then mix in some chlorine, phosphorus, fat, iron, sulfur, and glycerin, and you can put it into a package that you can carry home in the trunk of your car. And then you go down into the basement and make yourself a new body. It's not quite that easy, even if that is what your body is made of. When you look at the way these things are put together, it is incredible. For instance, you've got a heart. At least you've got serious problems if you don't have a heart.

I have a heart. I definitely know that because I had a medical procedure not too long ago where they opened my arm up and stuck something in a vein, and they sent a little thing inside, squirted some material in, and took some pictures. I actually saw my heart beating on the television screen. It was a tremendous relief to me, because people always say to me, "Stuart, have a heart." Now, my heart is a slow beating heart; it normally beats at forty-eight beats a minute. The average is seventy-two, which proves I'm slow.

I was reading about John Glenn, the first astronaut from America, the first astronaut to circle in space. When he was sitting in his little capsule on top of the great big rocket, do you know that his heart was beating at seventy-two to the minute? But when they blasted off, what do you think happened to his heart? It went on beating at seventy-two to the minute. And when he rode in space and was orbiting around there, the first American ever to do it (you can imagine how excited he was), his heart was going crazy at seventy-two beats a minute. That guy has got some heart.

Why does it keep beating? It keeps beating because it has to get five to six quarts of blood per minute circulating in our bodies. And do you know how long it takes, how many times your heart will beat in your lifetime, an average lifetime? One hundred billion times. It will pump enough blood to fill a New York skyscraper. You *are* fearfully and wonderfully made. When you learn these things, you're supposed to say, "Wow! God's smart, he's great. He makes bodies like that."

You've got a liver. Your liver performs more than five hundred entirely different functions, and it only weighs three pounds. It processes millions of dead blood cells every second. Just imagine how much work your liver has done since you started reading this book, and you haven't thought of it once. You've never even said, "Thank you, liver, for what you've done." You'd be in a mess without your liver and your blood. Every cubic millimeter of your blood contains five million red and up to ten thousand white cells. Two million of those red cells get damaged every second and need to be replaced. This blood carries the oxygen that your body needs all around your body. But if it carried the oxygen around as gas, bubbles would get in and things would go wrong. So it carries it around as tiny little solids and then has the ability to change it all. And when you exercise vigorously, seventy-five gallons of blood circulate per hour in your body, through one hundred thousand miles of blood vessels in your body. And everything goes around your circulatory system in twenty-six seconds. Let's all thank blood. No, let's thank God that we are fearfully and wonderfully made.

And then your kidneys, wonderful kidneys. You know you've got two of them. They each contain 140 miles of capillaries. They clean the waste from the equivalent of a ton of blood in your body every single day in order to maintain the critical mineral balance without which you cannot stay healthy. There is so much that is fascinating about the body.

One of my surgeon friends says I am just a frustrated surgeon, that that's what I'd be if I could be what I really wanted to be. That's not true; I am what I want to be. But I get so excited about the body because it reminds me of who made it. I am fearfully and wonderfully made.

The body, soul, and spirit interrelate

The second thing to remember about the design of the body is that your body and your soul and your spirit are all interrelated. Some people say there are two parts, body and soul, and others say there are three parts, body, soul, and spirit. And you can argue both ways from the Bible. For the sake of argument right now, let's look at 1 Thessalonians 5:23, which talks about body, soul, and spirit: "May your whole spirit, soul and body be kept blameless at the coming of our Lord Jesus Christ." This wonderful body of ours is made out of the most ordinary things, but also made into the most remarkable piece of machinery. Immediately, this body is also linked to your soul or spirit that makes you a person. You're not just a body; you're a person. And the link between your body and your soul/spirit is something that is a wonder to behold.

If you want to get to know me, how would you go about it? "Well," you say, "he's a very bad-tempered person." How do you know I'm bad-tempered? "Because," you say, "I remember once talking to him and his face went very red, the tiny little muscles around his eyes contracted, his eyes closed, and I could see a vein on his head and his neck really pulsing. I realized his blood pressure was going up, and he opened his mouth and yelled at me." What was it that helped you to get to know me, that I'm such a bad-tempered person? It's my body. How else are you going to get to know me?

I was talking to somebody the other day, and he really got after me. In the end he suddenly stopped and said, "I perceive you are angry with me." He was dead right. And I said, "You're dead right." And we had a little discussion about it. How did he know? Because he was able to see the way my body was reacting and demonstrating what my spirit/soul was feeling, thinking, and deciding. You see, we're all mixed up—body, soul, spirit—wonderfully made.

Of course, your body isn't just communicating bad things, either. One day I was at Milwaukee Airport, waiting for a plane to come in, and I saw my friend Junior Bridgman, who used to play for the Milwaukee Bucks. We talked as we waited. He was waiting for his wife and kids, who were flying in from Louisville, Kentucky. And I said to him, "Junior, oh, by the way, let me just explain something to you. In a few minutes, when the plane comes in, a tall, slim, gorgeous blue-eyed blonde, about twenty-six years of age, is going to come off this plane, run up to me, put her arms around my neck, and kiss me. . . . Junior, you have to believe me; it's my daughter." And he said, "Sure! Sure!" Well, of course it was my daughter, and I persuaded him that it really was my daughter. But when this blonde with the blue eyes comes and hugs me and kisses me, what's she saying? She's saying, "Dad, it's great to see you. I love you." But how do I know that? Her body.

We shake hands, we put our arms around each other, we hug each other, and we kiss each other. With our bodies we express who we are. The Bible says we are fearfully and wonderfully made, and our body, linked up with our spirit/soul, demonstrates and communicates what we are as a person. Our body is the means of expressing behavior that brings delight and glory to God.

The dangers of the body

In all fairness to our bodies, and in all fairness to you, I've also got to add that we need to be aware of the dangers of the body, too. Proverbs 23, along with many other passages of Scripture, goes into great detail about the dangers of the body. We all have legitimate appetites that God has put into our bodies because if they weren't there, your body wouldn't function and you wouldn't be around anymore. Legitimate appetites have to be used properly. If you eat stuff that you shouldn't be eating, or if you eat more stuff than you should be eating, you will cause damage to your body. If you damage your body, then, in effect, you are damaging yourself, the self that is intended to glorify God. There's a terrible danger for us to take the appetites that God has given to us—the appetites for food, for drink, for fellowship, for sex—and abuse them. And we need to be very careful about the abuses of the body.

As the apostle Paul says in Romans 1, we can use our bodies in such a way that is so contrary to what God demands that we not only degrade ourselves, but we degrade each other. Our society today needs to be aware of the fact that our bodies, which have legitimate appetites, unless they are properly disciplined, can be the means of bringing desperate degradation to us and to the other people who come into contact with our bodies and the degrading practices.

We also have to recognize that our bodies are the center of a tremendous spiritual conflict. You see, inside us and wanting to use our bodies, is an old selfish or sinful nature. But when we give our lives to Christ, Jesus Christ by his Spirit comes into our lives, and then something happens. It's like two opposing forces are at work in our bodies, and our bodies become a battlefield. You know what I mean. There have been times when you have been in a particular situation and you've thought to yourself, *I want to say that thing.* But something inside you says, *You shouldn't say that thing,* and something else inside you says, *I'm going to say that thing.* Then the other part of you says, *You will really be in trouble if you say that thing.* And the other side says, *I'm going to say it anyway.* So you went ahead and said it. But it was only after there was a conflict within you, in your body. So we need to recognize that this body of ours is wonderfully designed, it is part of us, and we are created to glorify God with it.

Yet, we have to recognize the dangers of the body not being properly used, which brings me to the discipline of the body.

The discipline of the body

In 1 Corinthians 9:24-27, the apostle Paul uses the picture of an athlete disciplining his body.

If an athlete is going to perform in a contest, he doesn't just show up: "Okay, I think I'll go and run the marathon today," and he takes the day off work and goes and runs the marathon. He wouldn't get anywhere. No, if he's going to run a marathon, he decides what the date of the marathon is that he will enter, and then he works back from that and decides how long he needs to go into strict training. He knows that if he's overweight, he's going to have to get rid of that excess weight. He knows that if he hasn't built up the

211

strength in his legs, he's going to have to do that. He knows that if he doesn't have the staying power and the stamina and his diet hasn't been right, he'd better get the staying power and the stamina and the diet right. In other words, he is going to go into training, and he is going to work meticulously in a disciplined way to get himself ready to run the race. That's exactly the picture that the apostle Paul uses.

Paul even goes so far as to say that he makes his body his slave, or his servant. In other words, he doesn't do any old thing his body wants to do, because his body is an expression of him, a communication of what is going on inside him. Therefore, if his body is doing all kinds of things that are clearly wrong and is clearly communicating things that are not to the glory of God, it shows what he's truly like. But if he is, under God and the power of his Spirit, disciplining his body, he will be demonstrating a disciplined life like a disciplined athlete. And that's what brings glory to God.

In Romans 12, Paul also says something else about his body. He says that he understood that it was possible for us to present our bodies as a living sacrifice to the Lord. In other words, he realized that the Lord Jesus can get hold of our bodies and use them as agents of his blessing.

We can say, in a sense, that it is like a skilled violinist getting hold of a violin and playing a magnificent tune. A great violinist, however, is not much good without a violin. And the great God looks for instruments, bodies, people who are prepared to commit themselves to him so they can play his music through their lives. Of course, if violins could kick and scream, they might say, "I don't like you scraping that thing over me, and I don't like all those piercing noises that are reverberating me. It gives me a headache, and so I'm not going to do it." But violins don't do that. They're just instruments.

We're more than instruments. We can say, "God, I don't want to do what you want me to do." We can say, "I don't like what is happening because of what you're doing in my life." But even then we come to the point of saying, "Lord, sometimes I don't like and sometimes I don't want to, but I will yield my body as a living sacrifice to you." That's the sort of thing he's asking us to do and that we need to be doing.

Paul also tells us in Romans 6 quite specifically that I can take individual parts of my body, and they can be instruments of righteousness or they can be instruments of unrighteousness. Let me give you a simple illustration. My hand is a pretty ordinary hand. It's been around sixty-three years. It obviously hasn't done much hard work. It isn't calloused like those of people who do a lot of manual work. It's a hand that's had much lighter work to do, but it can do all kinds of things. And it's possible for this hand to get hold of people who are really upset and just pat them. It's possible for this hand of mine to turn into a fist and sock people. I'm not a fighter; I've never done it, but it's possible. It is possible for this hand of mine to be an instrument of righteousness or an instrument of unrighteousness.

That's true of all the members of your body. What do you use your mouth for? What do you use your eyes, your ears, the members of your body for? Are they instruments of righteousness or instruments of unrighteousness? The apostle Paul says the discipline of the body requires me to be prepared to make my body a living sacrifice, to keep my body disciplined like an athlete and to make sure I'm presenting it as an instrument of righteousness.

Having said all that, the day comes when my life, my body, begins to deteriorate. I realized my body was deteriorating one day when my kids, whom I'd taught to run, were faster than I was. I used to go running with them, and they always tried to beat me and couldn't. Once, after being on a trip, my oldest son said, "Let's go and run a mile or two, Dad." And we'd just played an hour of racquetball!

I said, "Okay." And so we went into the gym and started running, and I shouted after him, "You're going too fast, Dave." He didn't take any notice, and I let him go. I figured I'd reel him in whenever I wanted to. And I wanted to and I didn't reel him in. He kept going and going and going, and he ran me right off my feet.

When we came to the end of the run, he kept going, and I was leaning up against the sides of the wall there panting and puffing. As he went past he said, "Come on, keep going, Dad; I don't like you letting me win."

I said, "Letting you win, what are you talking about? Come here, let me talk to you. What's been happening while I've been gone?"

He said, "Oh, I forgot to tell you; I'm on the cross country team." I suddenly felt my old body was deteriorating and this young guy was younger and fitter and sharper and stronger than I was, and that's how it goes. My hair's dropping out. My beard's turning whiter. People who have been to see the latest Indiana Jones movie are saying how much I look like Sean Connery. They're wrong. He looks like me. They even say I talk like him. He's Scottish, I'm English. But he's getting older too. No more James Bond for him or me. That's how it goes.

And you know, this deterioration of the body goes on until one day, the Bible says, "the deterioration of your body will come to such a point that your body will return to dust, *and your spirit to the God who made you.*" There's the critical point: Your body will return to dust, and your spirit to the God who made it. So you move in two directions now. They put your body in the grave, and it returns to dust. And your spirit/soul that inhabited that body, that needed the body to express itself, suddenly goes to the God who made it—without its body. And do you know what that's called? Death. And it happens to everybody sooner or later. So everybody has to think about it. Even young people need to think about it. Maybe your grandma or grandpa died. Were you ever able to talk to your parents about it? Were your parents able to talk intelligently and helpfully about it? Maybe they heard about a young person in an accident who died. Were you able to explain to them that the body returns to dust and the spirit returns to God who made it?

Understanding Death

People have got all kinds of ideas about death. The old philosophers who didn't know the Christian gospel said some awful things about death. Aristotle said, "Death is the most terrible of all things, for it is the end." Epicurus said a similar thing: "Death is the most terrifying of all things." Sophocles said, "Of all the great wonders, none is greater than man. Only for death can he find no cure." We can't, folks. We can't find a cure for death. There comes a time when the deterioration of this wonderful body that has been so magnificent, that we've really cared for and that we've understood and used properly, we hope, begins to deteriorate, and in the end we die. And wonderful man, who can do all kinds of wonderful things, can't do one thing. He can't find a cure for death. So what do we do about it? We try to pretend it doesn't happen.

Steve Brown is a pastor in Miami, Florida. Usually when you get on the plane in Miami, it's full of people who've been on a cruise. And people who've been on a cruise are usually wild, because they go on a cruise to be wild. They haven't quite got it all out of their system. So, Steve was on this plane. They were all celebrating, having a big party. But Steve noticed that the young woman sitting right across the aisle from him was having some difficulty. Eventually it was obvious that she was having severe difficulties. They asked if there was a doctor on the plane. Three doctors came and worked with her, and she died right there on the plane in the middle of the after-cruise party. Death suddenly came to the plane.

The mood changed immediately. They made an emergency landing in Dallas. They took the body of the young woman off the plane. And then they all got back on the plane and took off. Steve Brown, the minister, went up to one of the cabin attendants and said, "I'm a minister, and if you need me to talk to any of the people, or if you'd like me to talk to all of the people about what has happened, I'll be very happy to help."

215

And she said, "Oh, I think everybody's okay. We've given them all free drinks, and that will make them feel better." And that's how we handle death. We give them all free drinks so they will feel better. Is that how you handle death? No. You recognize that a dramatic thing has taken place. As the apostle Paul put it, believers who die are away from their bodies and at home with their Lord.

But what's going to happen? Are they just going to float around as disembodied beings in the presence of the Lord? You need the body to express yourself, to communicate yourself. If you're going to know who I am, or how I feel, or what I'm like, it's the body that's going to do it for you. So if I'm dying and my spirit/soul is with the Lord and my body is somewhere or other, returned to dust, how can I express myself in the presence of the Lord? This is what we call the intermediate state. It's a state that we don't altogether understand. There are all kinds of theories about it. Some people say, "The soul goes to sleep and is in an unconscious state, sort of waiting."

The Roman Catholic church teaches that there is a state called purgatory, which is a place of temporal punishment for those who die at peace with the church but less than perfect. They endure purifying suffering before they go to heaven. But you can make gifts, and prayers, and you can have masses that can shorten, alleviate, or even eliminate their sojourn in purgatory. Protestants don't believe that. If you ask Catholics, "Where do you get that from?" they will turn, if they know the Scriptures, to a section that we call the Apocrypha to the book of 2 Maccabees. That isn't in the Protestant Bible. There is no biblical warrant, the Protestants would say, for a belief in purgatory. We say that our eternal destiny is determined before we die, not after we die and go through all kinds of other procedures.

Other people say, "Reincarnation; that's what happens. The spirit leaves the body and then simply comes into another body, and you live your life all over again." Some people, like Shirley MacLaine, would try and tell you that John the Baptist was a reincarnation of

Elijah the prophet. And if you read your Bible, there are three things in there that sound like it, where people said of John the Baptist, "This is Elijah." Reincarnation theory is that the spirit leaves the body and then goes to another body after death. There's only one problem with that, and that is, Elijah didn't die. If you check, he didn't die. Also, when Elijah appears on the Mount of Transfiguration with the Lord Jesus, John the Baptist is already dead. So he couldn't have been a reincarnation. So there is no biblical warrant for believing in reincarnation.

When death comes, my body is returned to the dust, and the spirit is returned. Is it asleep? Is it going through purgatory? Is it in reincarnational process? I don't believe it's any of those. I believe that the body is returning to the dust, the spirit/soul is in the conscious presence of the Lord, but is waiting for a great triumphant day when God will raise everybody in newness of life and give them new bodies. And that is what we mean when we say, "I believe in the resurrection of the body."

It is called, in Romans 8:23, the redemption of the body. When you think about it, it's necessary, because sin has done all kinds of things to human beings, including making a terrible mess of their bodies. So, redemption is going to deal with their bodies too. All the effects of sin on our bodies, our spirits, and our souls have got to be totally dealt with if our salvation, our redemption, is totally complete. Therefore, our salvation, our redemption, is going to be thoroughly completed when the old body that has died is replaced with a new body, without any touch or taint of sin whatsoever.

Understanding the Resurrection

When Paul talks about the resurrection of the body in 1 Corinthians 15, his audience is a bit skeptical. They say, "Ahh, come on; you've got to be kidding." They ask him questions such as, "How are the dead raised, then? You mean to say that God is going to go around and scrape together all the dust that belongs to everybody's body and he's going to figure out, well, this belonged to him and this belonged to her? There are millions of people who've died, so how can he figure out all the dust?"

Someone said to me on one occasion, "You don't really believe that, do you? What happens if a missionary was eaten by a cannibal and then the cannibal dies. Whose dust is what?" That's a good point, isn't it? That's why we have people with Ph.D.s to answer questions like that.

The question is, How are the dead raised? The answer is, We don't know altogether, but notice that Paul talks about it in the great chapter that teaches the resurrection of Jesus from the dead. God will raise up new bodies; whether it is scraping together the dust of the original body and refashioning it, or whether it is giving a new one, I don't know. But we believe that he's going to do something of this nature for one reason only, because he raised up Christ from the dead, and we know that he did it.

The other question that skeptical people were asking Paul was, "What kind of body will they have?" And Paul says, when you put your body into the ground, it decays—like a seed. When you put a seed into the ground, it decays. But out of that death comes a little shoot, and out of that little shoot comes a stalk, and out of that stalk comes a plant, and out of that plant comes a flower, and out of that flower come many, many grains of seed. You put a seed in, but what comes out of it is totally different and yet totally the same. The body that is sown in death is going to be replaced by a new one that is going to be as different from the old one as the plant is from the seed. And yet it's going to be as similar as the plant is to seed.

Some people say it's going to be like Christ's body when he rose again from the dead. And that's a good point. It's going to be like his glorious body, Paul says in Philippians. Some people have said, "He died when he was thirty-three, so that means that we're all going to have thirty-three-year-old bodies in heaven." And twenty-one-year-olds say, "Oh." And fifty-eight-year-olds say, "Amen! I can't wait." We don't know.

But when this body of ours, new or the old one refashioned, is raised and reunited with our spirit/soul, we do know what's going to happen. In the presence of Christ and his Father, we will be uniquely equipped to be totally redeemed persons, seated for eternity in the presence of God, able to express ourselves, utterly forgiven, thoroughly whole, utterly liberated. That's what heaven is like. And believers are going to be there for all eternity.

So, says the apostle Paul, where is death's victory? That's a great question. Was Aristotle right—"Death is the most terrible of all things, for it is the end"? With all due respect to Aristotle, he was dead wrong. Death is not the most terrible of all things for the believer, for it is not the end. His body will go to dust, his spirit will go to the God who made it, and one day there will be a great resurrection day when God will reunite that liberated spirit with a body ideally suited to the new environment and he will have the opportunity of expressing himself in relationship to God in an eternal environment forever and ever.

So, says the apostle Paul, there is nothing to be frightened of in death. Death has no more sting. Death has no more victory. Then he comes up with a practical application of all this. He says, "Therefore, encourage each other with these things." It really is an encouraging thing to believe in the resurrection of the body. Because what it means is that you live carefully with the body you've got now, recognizing what it's designed for, recognizing the potential dangers of it, recognizing the necessity of discipline. You thoroughly understand its deterioration, but know what is happening in the deterioration process. You know exactly that it will return to dust, that the spirit will return to the God who made it, and it's only a matter of eternity, not a matter of time, until the new body fits you for active, glorious life in a totally new sphere.

Death isn't the end; it's a brief passageway into unspeakable glory. Therefore, encourage one another with these things. Paul's teaching, of course, is for believers only, people committed to Christ. Those who have not committed themselves to Christ have chosen to live their lives independently of God, and God chooses not to infringe upon their liberty. He will allow them to continue for eternity, independent of him. That's an awful thought.

MAKING IT PRACTICAL

1. What are some of "the dangers of the body"?

2. What does the Bible say happens to our body when we die?

3. Why is the resurrection of the body necessary? What does it really mean?

4. How do you respond to the idea of the resurrection of the body?

15

"The Life Everlasting"

Mark 10:17-30

There's an interesting little phrase in the Old Testament that I've often thought about. It says that God has set eternity in people's hearts. I've seen various interpretations of this, various ideas as to what it means. Let me make a suggestion to you: that there is within every human being a longing for something wonderful and beautiful and glorious that will never end.

I sense that this is the case because I remember as a little boy being read fairy tales. I hope that you tell your children fairy tales occasionally. I always used to wonder, *Why do fairy tales always start with "Once upon a time?"* Nobody else ever talked like that, and I'm not sure what it meant either. I also noticed that they usually finished with the expression "and they all lived happily ever after." The idea in the fairy tales that we tell to our children is that somehow or other everybody lives happily ever after. That desire is eternity set in our hearts.

A young couple fall in love. They want to express their love to each other. How do they do it? Often they do it in terms of "I will always love you." Notice the *always*. Or, if they really feel dramatic, "I will love you forever and ever." The quality of their love almost seems to be described in terms of quantity. It is an "always" love. It is a "forever and ever" love. There is the desire for that which is wonderful and beautiful and glorious to go on and on and on.

Think of the greatest vacation you ever had. Don't think about it too long because I may not get you back again! Think about it briefly. What happened when you discovered that you were running out of vacation? You said to yourself or you said to whoever you were with, "I just wish this would never end." Eternity in your hearts.

Of course, kids don't talk like this; they live much more circumscribed lives. But when Mother says, "Come on kids, bedtime," what is the kids' reaction? They don't want it to go on forever and ever because they're not thinking in those terms. Instead, they will give anything for ten more minutes.

"Just ten more minutes, Mom. Just ten more minutes."

"No, come on, it's bedtime."

"Five minutes, Mom. Just five minutes."

"No, it's your bedtime."

"Three, Mom. Just give me three minutes, and I promise I'll do my chores and I promise I'll always be good. Just one minute, Mom, just one minute."

What is it? They want to perpetuate that which is good. When you eventually get the little rascals into bed, fifteen drinks of water are necessary before they go to sleep. Why? Because they're enjoying what they're enjoying, and they don't want it ever to end. Eternity in our hearts.

There is something about our humanity that longs for the good and the beautiful and the glorious to go on and on and on. And it should come as no surprise to us, therefore, that God, having put this desire within us, is open to meeting the desire. There *is* such a thing as life everlasting. With that in mind, let's find out what the Scripture has to say about it.

First of all, how is life everlasting explained? Secondly, how is life everlasting experienced? And thirdly, how is life everlasting expressed?

What Does It Mean?

How is life everlasting explained? Sometimes you find in your Bible the word *eternal*, and sometimes you find the word *everlasting*. They both translate the same Greek word, *aiōnios*. We get the English words *aeon* and *age* from the first part of that Greek word. *Aiōnios* means, literally, "pertaining to an age." When we think in terms of everlasting life, we tend to think in terms of quantity, that is, life that goes on and on and on. That is a valid concept, but it is not the primary concept. The primary concept of life, which is *aiōnios* life eternal, is that it is pertaining to an age yet to come.

In Galatians 1:4 the apostle Paul talks about God wanting to deliver us from "the present evil age." The age that he's talking about is the era in which we live. We now live in this era that he characterizes as evil. And I don't suppose anybody's really going to get into an argument about there being something evil, something sinful about the world in which we live.

Paul, however, teaches, and Jesus also taught, that in addition to the present evil world, there is an age or a world to come. It is sometimes translated "age," sometimes translated "world." This age is in total contrast to the present evil age. It is not present; it is future. It will be introduced at the return of Christ, when in great glory he comes and establishes his eternal kingdom. It is not evil, for it will be characterized by goodness and righteousness and truth.

Secondly, I want to refer you to the passage in Mark 10. Let me just go through this rather familiar story with you quickly. The young man comes to Jesus in front of the whole crowd, kneels before him, and says, "Good Teacher, what must I do to inherit eternal life?" Jesus immediately picks up on the adjective *good* and says, "Why do you call me good? No one is good—except God alone." Put that in the back of your mind for a minute. He then goes on to answer the question "What must I do to inherit eternal life?" by saying, "You know the commandments: Do not murder, etc.,

etc." And the young man replies, "Teacher, all these I have kept since I was a boy." Jesus looks at him and says, "One thing you lack." And then to the utter amazement of everybody, not least the young man, he says, "Go, sell everything you have and give to the poor, and you will have treasure in heaven. Then come, follow me."

Many people reading this superficially have said, "Good night! You mean to tell me that if I want to inherit eternal life, the only way I can do it is by getting all my goods, putting them up for auction, selling them all off, getting all the money, giving it all away, and going into a monastery? Is that the way you inherit eternal life? That is what you would come to if you read this story superficially. Read on, however, and you will notice that the Lord Jesus goes on to say, as the young man walks away, how hard it is for the rich to enter the kingdom of God. The disciples were amazed at his words, but Jesus said again, "How hard it is to enter the kingdom of God." The disciples then said to each other, "Who then can be saved?"

Notice three expressions: the young man asks about inheriting eternal life, Jesus talks about entering the kingdom of God, and the disciples talk about being saved. But if you look carefully at this passage of Scripture, you'll find that they're all talking about the same thing. This helps us understand what it means to inherit eternal life. It is the same as entering the kingdom. The kingdom of God is that area of human experience in which God rules and reigns as king. The age to come will be characterized by God's rule and reign over everything. To inherit eternal life is the same as entering into a relationship with God, where he rules and reigns in your life.

One of the most common ways of expressing this, in bygone ages, was "being saved." People would ask other people, "Have you been saved? Are you saved?" Today that expression has gone out of vogue; now it's "born again." "When were you born again?" people ask one another.

This is something that will trigger a lot of people's antagonism and reaction. They don't like it. Those words are related to Jim

Bakker and Jimmy Swaggart, and they say that those born agains are just a bunch of hypocrites. But it's a perfectly valid biblical expression. It is perfectly appropriate to ask people, "Are you saved? Are you born again?" But I want to suggest, because of the connotations of these terms, that it might be more appropriate to ask on the basis of what Scripture says, "Do you know that you have eternal life?" It is the same as being saved; it is the same as entering into an experience where God rules and reigns in your life.

Notice the expression "being saved." The Lord Jesus expresses it this way: "It is easier for a camel to go through the eye of a needle than for a rich man to enter the kingdom of God" (verse 25). Jesus did say some wild things at times, didn't he? And here's one of the wildest.

You've probably heard some preachers use this illustration: In the East, in the ancient days, there were cities with walls around them, and all these big cities had a main gate. The gate would open early in the morning for all the commerce and all the farmers going in and out. In the evening it would be closed, and that made the city intact, safe. But there was beside the main gate a tiny little gate that latecomers could use if the watchmen would open it for them. However, if you had a camel with you and it was loaded with equipment, it was impossible for your camel to walk through this gate. So you'd have to get the camel to kneel down, unload everything, and push the thing through on its knees, and that's what Jesus meant. I've heard preachers preach that over and over again. And there's only one thing you can say about it. It's a great story, and it's wrong. There is no evidence at all that that little gate was ever called the eye of a needle.

The disciples then ask, "Who then can be saved?" And Jesus replies, "With man this is impossible, but not with God; all things are possible with God" (verses 26-27). There is as much chance of a human being entering the kingdom of God, receiving eternal life, being saved by their own efforts, as there is of you getting a full-grown camel through a little eye of a needle. What chance is there? *Zilch!* There is no way that a human being can be saved, can enter the kingdom, can inherit eternal life through his own efforts. The good news, however, is that with God it is possible. Jesus reminds us again that salvation, eternal life, the kingdom of God, are the results of God's grace extended to us, to give us what we do not deserve.

The fourth thing that helps us describe the life everlasting is that it is set in contrast to the term *perishing*. John 3:16 (KJV) says, "God so loved the world, that he gave his only begotten Son, that whosoever believeth in him should not perish, but have everlasting life." What does the term *perish* mean? There are one or two examples of comparisons in Scripture that help. For instance, Jesus said, "Don't spend your time working for meat that perishes." Before the age of refrigeration, meat would rot. It would perish. There was a slow deterioration. Perishing is something that happens in people's lives while they're still alive.

Paul, writing to the Corinthians, said this: "The message of the Cross to those who are perishing is foolishness." It is possible for a person to be like meat that is deteriorating, for there to be a moral deterioration that is slow, invisible, insidious, and relentless. That's one meaning of perishing.

Jesus gave another illustration of perishing. He said you never put new wine in old wineskins. He was talking about leather wineskins, which, if they were very old, would split. He said they would perish. When you've got leather or rubber or something like that, there is a slow disintegration. Perishing is not only a slow deterioration; it is a slow disintegration. The modern expressions would be, "My life is coming apart at the seams; the wheel came off; I'm trying to find myself."

If you don't like the word *perish*, how about the word *lost?* When the Prodigal Son eventually returned home, his older brother, who was a real sourpuss about the whole thing, was rebuked by the father. And the father said to him, "Rejoice with me! This, my son, was lost and is found." *Lost,* or *perishing,* means to be alienated, estranged from God, which leads to only a slow moral deterioration, which leads eventually to the disintegration of life. This process, if it is not arrested, leads to a final, irrevocable state where I am finally alienated from God, where my life does not have the moral content that is acceptable to God, and I have come to the point where my wheel has come off eternally. That's the bad news.

The good news is that life eternal is the exact opposite of perishing. Instead of being alienated from God, we go on to notice that life eternal is described as knowing God and his Son, Jesus Christ. This was the expression Jesus used, recorded in John 17:3: "This is eternal life: that they may know you, the only true God, and Jesus Christ, whom you have sent." Know them in what sense? Know them as God, know them as Lord, know them as Savior in an intimate, personal way.

Put all that together. When you know God, you're not alienated from him; you're not perishing. When you know God, he establishes his kingdom in your life and Christ is your Lord. When Christ is your Lord, you begin to experience his life, which is the life of the age to come. So you begin to discover while you are still alive that you're in touch with God, with eternity, with goodness and righteousness and truth in the here and now. You're beginning to enjoy the sweet by and by. When I say, "I believe in life everlasting," that's what I am talking about. It is a mind-blowing concept.

How Is It Experienced?

The question now that will come to mind, I suppose, is, how is the life everlasting experienced? There are two things I want to tell you about this.

It cannot be earned

First of all, we experience life everlasting by recognizing that it cannot be earned. When the young man came to talk to Jesus and said "Good Teacher," Jesus immediately took him up on the word *good* and said, "Why do you call me good? No one is good—except God alone" (verse 18). Why did he say that to him? I think the

227

reason was simply this, that when this young man looks at his life and the way that he's kept the Ten Commandments, as he thinks, this young man feels he's pretty good. In fact, he feels that he's good enough. When the Lord Jesus begins to go through the Ten Commandments with him, he nods his head and says, "I've kept all these." Then Jesus socks it to him and says, "All right, go and sell your goods, give the money away, etc., etc.," and he puts his finger on the sore spot. The sore spot is one of the Ten Commandments: Thou shalt not covet. And this young guy is riddled with covetousness. What is the point Jesus is making? There is none good but God; even those who think they've kept the commandments haven't. And even if they had, they still wouldn't have it in themselves to be all that is necessary to merit eternal life.

You see, the lesson we've got to get across that is so hard for people to understand is that to inherit eternal life, we must be perfect always. Just supposing you were to go to a friend, somebody that you really know, somebody that you've really developed a credibility with and you've earned the right to talk to them about deep spiritual issues, and say, "Can I ask you, as a good friend of mine, a very important question?" And they say, "Of course you can, you're my friend." Here's the question: "Do you know that you have eternal life?" That would be a very gracious way of doing it.

I'll guarantee you will find a wide variety of answers. Somebody might say, "I would never be that arrogant. I wouldn't have the audacity to stand here, look you in the face, and say that I have eternal life." And you say, "Why ever not?" And then you point out to them that you're not arrogant for knowing that you have eternal life for one simple reason: God says you can know that you have eternal life, and it's not arrogant to believe what God says. Then you respectfully point out to your friend that you're not the one who's arrogant, that your friend is the one who's arrogant. It is not arrogant to believe God; it is arrogant to know better than God. For God says, "These things are written that you might know that you have eternal life." What God says you can know.

When someone gives you that answer, what they're really saying is this: "I won't presume that I have been good enough to know that I have eternal life." Stated in simple terms, they're saying, "You've got to be good enough"—which is the same old philosophy.

Or you'll talk to somebody else and they'll say, "I guess I'm just going to leave it to the man upstairs. And when I stand before him, I guess he's going to bring out all the good things I did and all the bad things I did, and I just hope the good things outweigh the bad things. I just hope I'll get it." That is a common response. Notice the difference between knowing that you have and hoping that you'll get. There's no similarity. But the underlying thought is the same. To inherit eternal life, you've got to be perfect, and there's as much chance of you being perfect and earning eternal life, if you'll pardon the expression, as there is in getting a camel through the eye of a needle. With man this is impossible, but the good news is, with God it is possible.

It is a gift

What then, has God done? "The wages of sin is death," says the apostle Paul, "but the gift of God is eternal life in Christ Jesus our Lord." Wages are what you earn; gifts are what you receive. The second thing we say about experiencing life everlasting is this: after we recognize that we cannot earn it, we must recognize that we can receive it as a gift.

Some time ago, I met one of my neighbors. We stopped and chatted for just a minute or two. He was going off fishing, and he said, "I was watching on television last Sunday morning and I thought to myself, *He's my neighbor. Either he's gone or I'm gone, and if I didn't see him on television I never would see him.*" That was a surprise to me. I had no idea that he was watching television. I was glad to hear it. He then surprised me further by saying, "Would you give me a copy of your new book and autograph it to me?"

"Sure." So I went straight back home and got a copy of the book (actually I didn't know which one he meant because I had three new ones, but I picked one that I thought might be usable), and I autographed it to him. Then I was gone and he was gone; I missed him for about three weeks. Then one day, I'd just come back in from my early morning run, and he was just going out for his early morning fish. He waved to me. And I said, "Hey, just a minute," and I picked up the book that I had got for him and I ran out and gave it to him.

"You remembered."

"Sure," I said.

"How much do I owe you?"

"Oh, three quarters of a million would cover it. . . . No, Bill, it's a gift."

What do you not do when you are given a gift? You don't ask, "What do I owe you?" The incredible truth of the matter is this: You cannot go to God and say, "God, would you give me eternal life, please, and just let me know what I owe you." The incredible truth is that it's been paid for. I paid for that book, by the way. It wasn't that it was a freebie. I paid for it, gladly. Eternal life is a gift; you don't pay for it. Somebody else has paid.

How do you experience eternal life? Jesus said, "He that hears my word and believes on him that sent me has everlasting life and shall not come into condemnation, but is passed from death to life." Pretty straightforward, isn't it? So the question we ask ourselves now is this: "All right, if I understand that eternal life is the life of the age to come, it is entering the kingdom, it is being saved, it is the opposite of perishing, it is knowing God, and it all happens when I admit that I cannot earn it or deserve it and receive it gladly as a gift, then how do I know that I've received the gift?

How Is the Life Everlasting Expressed?

There are two main ways of looking at this. Let me touch on them very briefly. From an attitudinal point of view, we can tell when we really know that we have eternal life. There is an attitude of calm, settled assurance. "These things have I written unto you that believe, that you may know that you have eternal life." Not arrogance, just humble trusting and thankfulness. There is an attitude of assurance.

Paul, writing to Timothy, says, "Lay hold of eternal life." It is the life to come, but you can begin to experience it now. Lay hold of it and live it to the full. Appreciation and anticipation are the characteristics of those who have eternal life. Jude, in his very brief epistle, tells us that we should be waiting for the mercy of the Lord that will bring us to eternal life. In other words, we live with keen anticipation of the life to come.

As Paul wrote to the Galatians, "If you sow to the sinful nature, you will of the sinful nature reap destruction." Remember the principle, "what you sow, you reap"? But then Paul says, "But if you sow to the Spirit, you'll reap life eternal." You will begin to experience the life of the age to come now in a preparatory sort of way, with glimmerings of ultimate glory as you apply the principles of the Spirit. And so the attitude of the person who has life everlasting is rather easy to identify: There's a serenity of assurance, a deep appreciation, and anticipation of the life to come. They live now in the light of *then*.

It is seen in behavior too. The Lord Jesus, speaking to the woman at the well, said this: "The water that I will give you will be in you like a well of water springing up to everlasting life." The word "springing up" there is the same word that describes the lame man who is healed outside the temple, who caused quite a stir by running into the temple, leaping and jumping and praising God. It's a picture of vitality, of vigor, of raw energy. You can tell people who are living in the light of everlasting life. They have hidden resources of spiritual strength. There is raw spiritual energy about them; they're vital; they're vivacious; they're living in the good of the life of the age to come because they acknowledge the Lordship of Christ, they rejoice in his saving grace, and they know the fullness of his Spirit.

The Bible says, "These things are written that you might know that you have eternal life." Do you know that you have eternal life? The great Charles Haddon Spurgeon on one occasion said to his congregation, "I want you all to go home. I want everyone of you to take a piece of paper, and I want you to write on the piece of paper either 'forgiven' or 'condemned.' " I've no idea how many of his congregation did it. I'd like to ask you to do this: Take a piece of paper and write on it, either "eternal life" or "perishing." Maybe you'd like to pray something like this:

Lord,

I guess I've always thought that somehow or other I could earn eternal life, but if I'm quite honest with myself, I haven't even been trying very hard to earn it. I've been trying to get the old camel through the eye of the needle. It's not difficult; it's impossible. But it is possible with you in my life, and because Christ died for me, you can give me what I don't deserve. I come humbly and repentantly to you, and I ask you for the gift of eternal life, on the understanding that I'll begin to experience it in this present evil age, as well as in the life of the age to come, and it will start to show. I'd like to thank you very much for hearing this prayer. And I'd like to thank you for all that lies ahead in time.
In Christ's name,
Amen

MAKING IT PRACTICAL

1. What does the Greek word meaning "everlasting" or "eternal" mean literally?

2. What is required in order for us to have eternal life? How can we know we have eternal life?

3. What practical evidence can help assure us that we do have everlasting life?

4. What is the significance of eternal life being contrasted with the word *perish* in John 3:16? What is the fuller meaning of the word *perish?*

16

"Amen"

Nehemiah 8:1-18

Amen is a Hebrew word that has found its way into many languages, particularly in the languages of worship and witness, although not exclusively so. For instance, one day when I was driving to work, one of these radio talk shows was on where there seem to be two or three people in the studio and they're doing the news and the weather and the sports and they're sort of chit-chatting about nothing much. They seemed to be agreeing on everything, and then one of them seemed to have gotten stuck on "Amen." So whenever anybody said something, he said, "Amen!" Of course there was nothing spiritual about it. It was just an affirmation. He was agreeing.

But when you move into the Christian world, you find that the word *Amen* is common usage. Awhile ago I was in Austria, where I spoke at a convention. There were over twenty different countries represented, and probably as many as fifteen languages. And we had all kinds of interpretation going on. I thought it would be good if every morning we started off with the things that we had in common. So I told them that there are three words that have the same usage in the Christian church wherever you go. And I got them to repeat these three words at the beginning of every talk. It gave us this feeling of solidarity. The first one was *Amen,* the second word was *Alleluia,* and the third word was *Coca-Cola.* These are the three universally used words, wherever the church of

Jesus Christ meets. Although I won't spend time discussing the other two words here, I do want to concentrate on this word *Amen*.

The meaning of Amen

The Hebrew, in its original form, means literally "that which is reliable, sure, or true." *Amen* was often used, and is still used, to conclude a prayer. A lot of people seem to think that *Amen* at the end of a prayer is sort of a Hebrew period: "That means he's stopped; now I can open my eyes." But it means considerably more than that.

When a person prays, and at the conclusion of their own prayer, says Amen, what they're really showing is strong affirmation: "This is really, truly what is in my heart." Of course, you'll find that it is appropriate in many church services when someone else leads the congregation in prayer or when you have a small group praying together, not only for the person doing the praying to say Amen, but for the others to articulate an Amen as well. When they do that, there's a sense that the group is agreeing. This is something that is very truly on their hearts.

Here's a story that was one of my favorites when I was a little boy. There was an Anglican vicar who was very concerned that when the people should have said Amen in the service, they weren't saying it. So he thought he'd get somebody planted in the congregation who would do it, and that would get everybody going. He got the caretaker (they call him the verger) to do it. The verger said, well, he didn't really know when to say Amen in the service. (And he'd only been going to church for about fifty-five years.) So, the vicar said, why don't you sit just below where I lead the service, and I will have a bag of dried peas in my hand. And every time you should say Amen, I will drop a dried pea on your bald head. It worked beautifully. For the first week he would say something in the liturgy and would drop a pea on the verger's head. The verger would say Amen, and the congregation would say Amen. Say something else, dried pea, bald head, Amen, Amen. Then one week he said Amen, Amen, Amen, Amen, and suddenly he went, "AmAmAmAmAmAmAmen"— the vicar's bag had burst. But let's face it, there is an appropriate time to say Amen. There is a time when at the conclusion of a prayer I should add my affirmation to what has been said.

But Paul didn't keep his Amen for just the conclusion. Sometimes in the middle of what he is saying he drops in an Amen. And not even in the middle. For instance, in Romans chapter 1, nowhere close to the end of the letter, he's saying a lot of serious things about human sin and depravity and how God is dealing with people, and then he talks about the glory of God. The Greek word for glory is *doxa*. And the appropriate response to a statement concerning the *doxa* of God is the Doxology, attributing praise to God for his glory. Whenever Paul gives mention to a doxology, he concludes it with Amen.

When Paul's letters were written, they weren't written just to be included in a Bible. They were letters written to people in a geographic location. So the Epistle to the Romans is a letter to some people who lived in Rome. And when they were gathered in church one morning, somebody would get up and say, "I just got a letter from Paul; do you want to read it?" And that was the first time the Epistle to the Romans was read. When they came, in Romans chapter 1, to the great statement with that great doxology, and it was concluded with Amen, that was a signal that the whole congregation would say Amen; They were all caught up in what was going on. So Amen is not only an individual statement of affirmation; it is also intended to be a corporate statement of affirmation.

Let me give you one or two examples of the usage of Amen. When King David decided that his son Solomon should be his successor, he called together a group of people who were responsible for getting young Solomon and anointing him as king. But there was a problem: Solomon's mother was Bathsheba. And you remember how David and Bathsheba first got together. So there would obviously be some reservation, I'm sure, on the part of some people as to whether Solomon, of all his sons, ought to be the king.

When David had to be confronted about his sin with Bathsheba, it was Nathan the prophet who did the confronting. Nathan was a gutsy guy if ever there was one. But I'm particularly intrigued to see that when David called a group of people together to anoint Solomon as the new king, Nathan was in that group. Whatever his reservations were, when he heard the command of the king, he and the other men (you've guessed it!) said Amen. And what that meant was, "Yes, your majesty, you've given us a royal edict, we heartily agree, and we will put it into practice." And that's another usage of the word *Amen*.

One of the things the people of Israel were going to do when they got to the Promised Land was to go to an area that we call Samaria, where there was a natural amphitheater. There were two mountains, Gerizim and Ebal, and the people were to be divided into two great congregations. One would stand on one mountain and one on the other. Those who stood on Mt. Gerizim would hear the priests recite all the blessings that God had promised them. And at the end of each blessing, with a great sound that would fill the amphitheater, they would say, "Amen!" The other half, on Mt. Ebal, were required to give a great resounding Amen not only to the blessings, but also the cursings—all the things they were told that would happen to them if they did not obey. This reminds us that Amen is an intelligent response to the divine truth whether it's palatable or not.

Then in the book of Psalms we find other examples of how Amen is used. There are 150 Psalms, but they are divided into four books. At the conclusion of each of the four books there is an instruction: "Let all the people praise thee, Amen and Amen." The book of Psalms is literally the hymnbook of the Hebrews, and at the end of each section of the hymns in the hymnbook, Amen is included. It is, therefore, perfectly appropriate for us to sing hymns, traditional and historical verifiable hymns that have theological content, and at the conclusion of singing these hymns to sing together a great Amen. And when we do that, we are simply making a corporate affirmation of the validity and truthfulness of the things that we are singing.

A young man came to me at the end of one of our services one Sunday. He said that he'd not been to our church before and that our form of worship was different from anything that he'd ever experienced. He added, "I was very resistant, but when the people started to sing, I found my resistance ebbing away. When I found them all corporately coming together, I found myself, almost against myself, being lifted up in praise. . . . I praised today like I've never done before in my life."

So, Amen is used at the end of Psalms, and it is appropriately used at the end of the hymns that we sing. The apostle Paul, writing to the Corinthian church, was very much concerned about the way they were abusing a particular gift—the gift of tongues—at that particular time. And so he gave them instructions as to how they should appropriately exercise this gift: "If somebody comes in and all you guys are speaking in tongues, he won't have a clue what you're talking about. . . . And if he doesn't know what you're talking about, how can he say Amen to what you're saying?" The inescapable inference is this: that somebody coming into a worship service can reasonably expect to understand what is going on, and it is reasonable for him, whenever it is an appropriate time, to say Amen because he intelligently appreciates what is being said.

Having said that, there are many churches where you'll never hear an Amen. And if somebody does let one rip, everybody looks at them as if they've done something inappropriate in church. On the other hand, there are churches where there's so much "Amen-ing" going on that it's difficult to get anything else done. I've been in all kinds of churches, and I want to say to you that when you get into a congregation where there is never a vocal affirmation of what is going on, it is reasonable to wonder if anything is going on! By the same token, when you get into a situation where there's so much "Amen-ing" going on that it's difficult to make sense of the service, one wonders if there's any intelligent thinking going on!

When I first came to America, the very first day, the very first week of my ministry in America over twenty-five years ago, I met a delightful Southern preacher. He was quite an elderly man at the time, while I was just a young guy. We hit it off together, and I really enjoyed him; we became friends. I had no idea what he was talking about most of the time, but he seemed to be a real genuine guy. And whenever I went into the deep South, years and years later, he would often show up in the church where I was preaching. I'd always know he was there because there'd be a resounding "Amen, Amen!" And he would be nudging people with his elbow, saying, "Did you hear that! Amen!" Well, that's great. I like that. At least somebody was in agreement with me, and they were listening. (At least I thought they were listening.)

On one occasion, when I was preaching in south Alabama, my friend was "Amen-ing" up a storm. In fact, he was doing much better than I was. So I thought, *I've got to shut him up some way or other.* I decided to say something totally wrong but with tremendous emphasis. When you really get the Amen corner going, if you say something with emphasis, that will usually get an Amen out of them. And if you say something *totally wrong* with emphasis, they will say Amen to heresy, and then you've got them. So that's what I did. And he came out with a big resounding Amen to total heresy. So I said, "Was that you?"

"Yes, yes," he replied.

"Do you know what you just said?"

"I said 'Amen.'"

"Do you know what you said it to?" I asked.

He said, "Uh, no."

"Well," I said, "You might be interested to know that you said it to heresy."

"Stop being impertinent," he replied. "Just go on preaching the Word, young man." But it shook him up, and that was good, because I'm not sure which is worse—people of God never saying "Amen and Amen," or people saying it but not knowing what they're saying it to. There is a place for the affirmation of truth, individually and corporately, and we need to recognize its significance.

Let me turn your attention to Nehemiah 8:1-3. And in this chapter, which, incidentally, is one of my favorite chapters of the Bible because it outlines my philosophy of preaching, we will find some information concerning people who were saying Amen in a worship experience. The children of Israel have been waiting in captivity, and now they're being restored to their ancient land, which lies in ruins. They've gone back to Jerusalem, which has been decimated, and the temple has been destroyed. They're about to rebuild. During the course of their return, they have discovered the long-forgotten and long-lost book of the Law, and they're excited about it.

So in Nehemiah 8:1-3 we read,

All the people assembled as one man in the square before the Water Gate. They told Ezra the scribe to bring out the Book of the Law of Moses, which the LORD had commanded for Israel.

So on the first day of the seventh month Ezra the priest brought the Law before the assembly, which was made up of men and women and all who were able to understand. He read it aloud from daybreak till noon as he faced the square before the Water Gate in the presence of the men, women, and others who could understand. And all the people listened attentively to the Book of the Law.

I love it. You see where I get my philosophy of preaching! People tell me, "Stuart, don't go on too long, because the mind cannot absorb what the seat cannot endure." Have you ever heard that? I always respond, "That just gives you some indication of where their minds are situated!"

What a wonderful thing it would be to have people who would listen attentively to the Word of God from daybreak until noon—and they didn't even have seats! They were standing. Ezra the scribe stood on a high wooden platform built for the occasion. Beside him, on his right hand, stood a number of very nice gentlemen with unpronounceable names. And on his left stood another number of gentlemen with equally unpronounceable names. Ezra opened the book. All the people could see him because he was standing above them. And as he opened it, the people all stood up. Ezra praised the Lord, the great God, and all the people lifted their hands and responded, "Amen and Amen." And they bowed down and worshipped the Lord with their faces to the ground.

Look now in chapter 9, verse 5. The same gentlemen whose names we cannot pronounce said, "Stand up and praise the LORD your God, who is from everlasting to everlasting." There are two aspects to what is going on here: There is a lot of praising, a lot of preaching, and they give careful attention to the preaching of the Word.

I want to suggest to you that the appropriate use of the word *Amen* is, first of all, a response to the praising, and secondly, a response to the preaching. There were some big promises being made by these people, and their response of Amen was appropriate to the promising that was going on as well. There are your three key words: *praising, preaching,* and *promising.*

A Response to Praise

The important thing about praise is that we should know to whom it is being directed when it is intended to constitute worship. Praise is directed toward God. We have just seen in Nehemiah 9:5 that the people were standing up and praising the Lord. It's an incredible thing to me to come into a service and to see people who are not participating in the praising that's going on. They're just standing there. All around them are literally hundreds of people who are singing their hearts out. People say, "I don't like singing," "I don't like this kind of music," or "I don't like that kind of music." That is totally beside the point. You are told to stand up and praise the Lord your

God. If you have an appropriate understanding of who the Lord God is, it is most inappropriate not to express praise to him.

Nehemiah chapter 9 mentions three specific things about the Lord their God. First of all, it says in verse 5, "Blessed be your glorious name, and may it be exalted above all blessing and praise. You alone are the Lord. You made the heavens." Then it goes on to talk about the Lord of creation. Anybody who has got any sense at all of creation ought to be able to articulate praise to the God of creation, who is listening. In verses 7 and 8 it says, "You are the LORD God, who chose Abram. . . . You found his heart faithful to you, and you made a covenant with him."

So he's not only the Lord of creation, but the Lord of covenant. Anybody who understands that God is a covenant-making and covenant-keeping God and knows that he or she has entered into a covenant relationship with God ought to have a heart of praise. As you go on a bit further, the Bible gives a brief and sad history of the people of Israel. God chooses them and blesses them and asks them to respond to him in loving obedience. They disobey, and he sends him prophets to warn them of the dire consequences of disobedience. They kill the prophets. The dire consequences of disobedience come, and they fall on hard times. They repent and God reaches out in compassion; they're restored, and they love the Lord their God.

Then he says, "Go show your love in obedience." Once again they are disobedient, so he sends his prophets. The people kill the prophets, and dire circumstances come again; they repent, and his compassion is shown—over and over and over again. Read it in Nehemiah 9. Creation, covenant, compassion. These are the dominant themes that elicit praise from the people of God when they understand who God is.

What a wonderful opportunity we've had in these previous 15 chapters to look very carefully into what we profess to believe. And the more we profess to believe it, the more we ask ourselves, Do I really believe it? If you believe these superlative truths of the

Christian faith, it is normal to expect praise to be part and parcel of your experience.

We direct our praise to the great God. Notice that this praise is an expression of worship. Some people seem to think that praise *is* worship. Praise is an aspect of worship. It is possible to worship without praising. But if you're truly praising the living God, that is part of worship.

Dr. Donald English, who's one of the finest Bible preachers I know anywhere in the world, said this: "Whenever I leave a worship service I ask myself, Which part of me need I not have brought here today?" And that's a good point, because to worship means that I bring my mind to bear on truth. I allow my emotions to be touched by truth. I make willing response to truth, and it requires my body to put this truth, this volitional response, this emotional response into action. We should never be in a position to say—"I came to worship this morning. I may as well have left my mind at home; there was no intelligent communication of truth at all. Or I should have left my emotions at home today because the truth was true, but it was as dull as ditch water. Or, it could be that there was absolutely nothing that galvanized me into response and I will simply go home the way I came."

Worship is a response of adoration in intelligent appreciation for who the Lord is and what he has done. That is why you don't just say, "I don't go to worship anymore because I don't get anything out of it." That is not the point. You go to worship because of an intelligent appreciation, an articulation of who God is, expressed in a variety of forms. Granted, the service should be so designed that you are stimulated to this, but the responsibility is on you to worship and to express appreciation for who he is and what he has done in your life.

Notice the varied styles of praise that seem to be appropriate in this situation. Praise can be spoken; we've already seen that. Praise should be sung, too. Ezra 3:10 says, "When the builders laid the foundation of the temple of the LORD, the priests in their vestments and with trumpets, and the Levites . . . with cymbals, took their places to praise the LORD." How were they praising the Lord? Well, a guy who could play his trumpet brought his trumpet along; a girl who could play her cymbals brought her cymbals along; and they were hooting and tooting and clashing and clanging, praising God.

Then, in verse 11, it says, "With praise and thanksgiving they sang to the LORD: 'He is good; his love to Israel endures forever.'" Notice what King David had prescribed as praise. I hear people say some strange things about music in worship, things like, "We should only use the piano and the organ." I can't find a piano anywhere in the Bible. I certainly haven't found a synthesizer in the Bible. But I have found all kinds of fascinating brass instruments, string instruments, percussion instruments . . . you name it, they are there. And it seems appropriate to me, if you can play an instrument, that you should bring it along and utilize it somehow or other in making some great big sound that is going to help people praise God. And sing, too.

The question is, What kind of music should we sing? Some people who talk about worship mean singing a lot of contemporary songs, one after the other. That may or may not be worship. There's a certain arrogance about some people in the church of Jesus Christ today who talk about contemporary singing as if that is worship and nothing else is. Why is it arrogant, you ask? Because it is suggesting that for eighteen centuries the church didn't know how to do it, and we have found out at last. We don't just sing contemporary music. We need to recognize that we have a great history and a great tradition, and that we are part of a communion of saints that goes from the first century all the way through.

But by the same token, there are some people who hate contemporary music. They feel it has no place in the church of Jesus Christ. What utter nonsense. That is to suggest that God stopped being creative in his people three centuries ago. Has God declared a moratorium on creativity? Isn't it appropriate to believe that God will take every kind of music in human history, in every era of society, and touch people's hearts and use it as a medium to praise him?

The great hymns of Luther were set to bar tunes. General William Booth of the Salvation Army said, "Why should the devil have all the best songs?" So he went in the pubs and got their songs and put Christian words to them. The hymns that we think are so holy and so wonderful started out in the beer halls of Münich and the pubs of England, many of them. And some of them came from Mozart and Haydn and Beethoven, whose lives don't always bear looking into either. We must begin to realize that there is a great eclecticism that is appropriate just so long as it is stimulating people in various mediums to give an intelligent articulation of their praise of God.

A Response to Preaching

Saying Amen to praising is most appropriate. Saying Amen to preaching is most appropriate, too. I love the statement on preaching in Nehemiah Chapter 8. The people were hungry for the Word of God, so they were the ones who said to Ezra, "Bring the Book."

One of the great things about Elmbrook is that over the years it has always been characterized by a hunger for the Word of God. And if our church ever loses its hunger for the Word of God and gets sidetracked into other things, then the key to our strength will be lost.

Notice, however, that it is not just that the people are hungry; also, the people whose responsibility it is to minister the Word are thoroughly prepared. Ezra, in chapter 7, verse 6 "was a teacher well versed in the Law of Moses, which the Lord, the God of Israel, had given. . . . [And] the hand of the Lord his God was on him." He had no business ministering the Word if those two things were not true. Not only that, it says, "Ezra had devoted himself to the study and observance of the Law of the Lord, and to teaching its decrees and laws in Israel" (verse 10). Ezra had devoted himself to studying it, to doing it, and to teaching it.

When you have a congregation comprised of people who are hungry for God's Word, people who are devoted to the Lord, people who know the hand of the Lord their God is upon them, people who will devote themselves to study and to practice and to teaching, God's Word can be released in mighty power—through people giving an intelligent Amen to what is being said.

There's no question that Ezra was the best-known preacher in the Jerusalem situation, but I want you to notice that Ezra was not the one who did all the preaching. All those gentlemen with unpronounceable names were deeply involved in the preaching too. A church should never become a community of people who come to hear a preacher, as opposed to hearing the preaching of the Word. The attitude of the people and the preparation of the preacher are both important. In Nehemiah 8:2 it says that those who were able to understand arrived there. And in verse 8 they read from the Book of the Law, making it clear, giving the meaning so that the people could understand.

It's one thing to get people who are able to, and it's another thing to get them to do it. The job of the preacher and the anointing of the Spirit is to get those who are perfectly capable of understanding to come to the point of really understanding the Word of the Lord. When the people come to the point of understanding it, then the preacher can lead them to the point of doing what they now understand. And that's what preaching is all about. You gather people who are capable of understanding, you minister to them in such a way that they do understand, and then you lead them into the application of it because they understand.

And there's my philosophy of preaching. That's what has kept me preaching all these years, all around the world. What I've tried to do is read from the Book of the Law of God, make it clear, give the meaning so that people can understand, and when they understand it, encourage them to do what they now understand. When that is taking place, people ought to be saying at the end of the preaching, "Amen."

At the end of one of our Sunday services, a delightful lady came to the microphone to express what God had been speaking to her about in the Apostles' Creed. She said what it was and then repeated the article from the Apostles' Creed.

I asked her, "Are you saying Amen to that?"

And she said, "You bet ya!"

I said, "The word is *Amen,* but 'you bet ya' will do."

Amen. Is that your response to the preaching? Is that your response to the praising?

A Response to Promises

At the end of chapter 9 of Nehemiah, when the people stand up to praise the Lord their God and listen to all the preaching, they say, "We are making a binding agreement, putting it in writing." To give you an idea of what was happening in Ezra and Nehemiah's time, let me identify for you in Nehemiah chapter 10 the sort of things that they were saying. In Nehemiah 10:30, the people say, "We promise . . . " In verse 31 they say, "We will not . . . " In verse 32, "We assume responsibility . . . " Verse 36, "We will bring . . . " Verse 39, "We will not neglect . . . " Do you get the picture? All these things that they are saying are a response to the praising and the preaching, for the promising is what is appropriate now. After they hear the preaching and say Amen, they make their promises and seal them with a great "Amen and Amen."

Can you say Amen?

MAKING IT PRACTICAL

1. To what three things is *Amen* an appropriate response?

2. In Nehemiah 9, what are the three dominant themes that elicit praise from God's people when they realize who he is?

3. What are the two dangerous extremes in our usage of the word *Amen?* To which does your church tend?

4. What will you do to show, through your life and your actions, your Amen, or your agreement with the Apostles' Creed?

Tapes Available

A complete set of audio-taped messages by Stuart Briscoe on The Apostles' Creed is available from:

> Telling the Truth
> Elmbrook Church
> 777 South Barker Road
> Waukesha, WI 53186
>
> 1-800-24-TRUTH
> 1-800-23-TRUTH (in Wisconsin)
> Fax: 414-796-5752

Christian Belief and the Modern World, Volume 1
   Album #38

Christian Belief and the Modern World, Volume 2
   Album #39